LOCHS & GLENS
of SCOTLAND

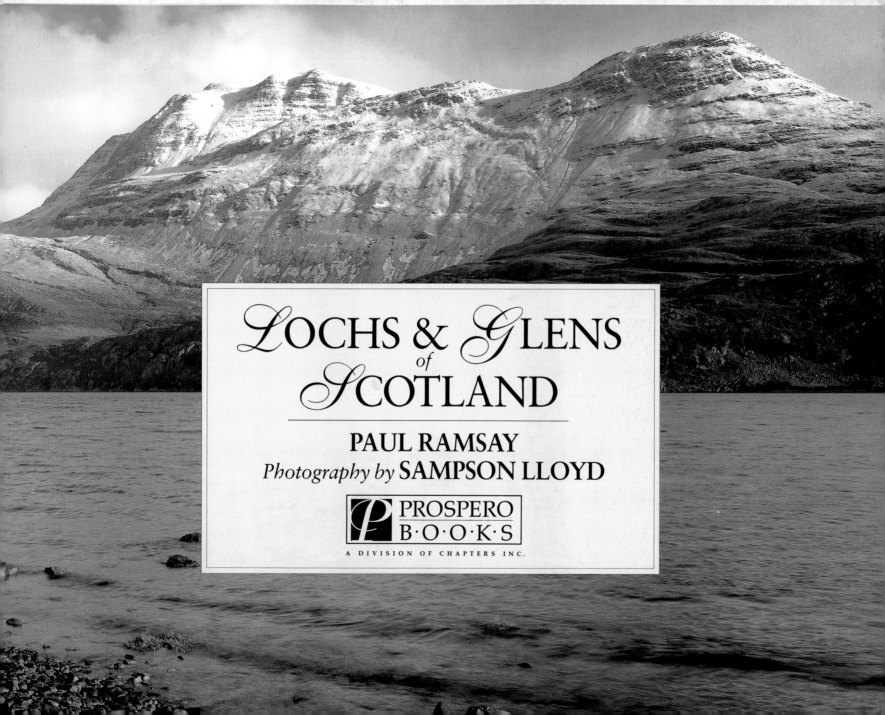

LOCHS & GLENS
of
SCOTLAND

PAUL RAMSAY

Photography by **SAMPSON LLOYD**

PROSPERO
B·O·O·K·S
A DIVISION OF CHAPTERS INC.

FRONT COVER: *Loch Assynt with Ardvreck Castle.*
BACK COVER: *Loch Laggan.*

FRONTISPIECE: *Loch Maree.*

First published in Great Britain in 1994
by Collins & Brown Limited
Letts of London House
Great Eastern Wharf
Parkgate Road
London SW11 4NQ

This edition produced for Prospero Books,
a division of Chapters Inc.

1 3 5 7 9 8 6 4 2

British Library Cataloguing-in-Publication Data:
A catalogue record for this book is available from the British Library.

ISBN 1 55267 991 8 (paperback edition)

Conceived, edited and designed by Collins & Brown Limited

Editor: Colin Ziegler
Art Director: Roger Bristow
Styled by: Ruth Hope
Designer: Clare Clements

Filmset by Textype Typesetters, Cambridge
Reproduction by Scantrans, Singapore
Printed and bound in Italy

Contents

$\mathcal{I}$NTRODUCTION

THE MUSIC OF THE PIPES resounds throughout the castle; a feast is being held in the vaulted hall. Sitting in his great chair at the head of the massive oak table the chief is splendid in tartan. The finest haggis, borne aloft on a silver ashet by a strapping Highlander, is taken round to 'Himself' and is slashed open with a dirk. The fumes of whisky eddy in the air, mingling with the music of the pipes and the mist of the dry ice. The chief and his lady are actors. The kilted gillies are employees of a catering organization; and the guests have come from Chicago, or Japan, or Germany. They have been presented with a version of the great Scottish myth, and perhaps they have enjoyed the experience.

What is this myth? Let us do a little free association. Highlands, heather, kilts, tartan, eagles, clans, salmon, Gaelic, pine trees, songs, massacres, Glencoe, King Robert, Bonnie Prince Charlie, Culloden, sheep, Clearances, crofters, red deer, Monarch of the Glen, Queen Victoria, Balmoral, Sir Walter Scott, Rob Roy, Rabbie Burns, whisky. That is enough. We are talking about a land and its people; 'The land of bens and glens and heroes', or lochs and glens.

Much of this book is about the past, but the results of the actions of our ancestors are still with us in the landscape today. It is necessary to know that what we see now was not always so. This book is an attempt to put Highland history into an environmental context, and to incorporate something of the Gaelic view of the country. From a knowledge of what these Highlands were we can go on to ask 'How might these Highlands be yet?'

The part played by the last ice age in moulding and sculpting the landscape, and directing and redirecting the flow of rivers and lochs has given us much of our scenery, but the underlying structure was determined by earlier geological history. To this we owe the slabby magnificence of the Torridonian sandstones found in the North-west Highlands, the rugged grandeur of Glencoe, the granite plateau of the

ACHMELVICH

A Sutherland sky-line looking south-east from Achmelvich on the coast, with Canisp to the north, Suilven in the middle and Cul Mor to the south. A gnarled and battered rowan seems almost to be growing out of the bare rock—the 2.8 billion year old Lewisian gneiss.

Cairngorms. The distinctive appearance of each stretch of country is due to the character of the underlying rocks. At Elphin in Sutherland, after travelling through wastes of peat and ancient rock and seeing those extraordinary sandstone structures Stac Pollaidh and Suilven, we come into a green haven, a patch of the limestone that outcrops from Durness on the north coast down to Skye. Further south, in Wester Ross, one can drive over the rugged desolation of the Bealach nam Bo, look across the Applecross peninsula, and come down to the jewel-like green of that ancient holy place, the sanctuary of Saint Maol Rubha, endowed with a more generous geology.

The Highlands are riven by many fault lines, the result of major upheavals, but the two best known are the Great Glen Fault, which separates the Northern Highlands from the Central Highlands and is the line along which Loch Ness, Loch Oich and Loch Lochy run, and the Great Highland Boundary Fault. This runs from Stonehaven in the north-east of Scotland down, in a south-westerly direction, to Helensburgh on the River Clyde. It separates a country dominated by the ancient, hard, mainly metamorphic rocks (dating back 2,800 million years in the case of the Lewisian gneiss), from the younger mainly sedimentary rocks of the Devonian era (359 to 370 million years ago); such as the Old Red Sandstones, famous for the fertile soils to which they give rise in Strathmore, the Laigh of Moray, Caithness and Orkney.

The geology and past climates of the Highlands have decreed a physiography in which the straths and glens of the east side of the country penetrate far over to the west; the watershed being sometimes only a handful of miles from the west coast. The line of the watershed, on the west side of the country, with its fast-flowing, short-running rivers, was called Drumalbyn (from Druim Albann meaning the back of Scotland) from as early as the seventh century AD. This was the approximate line of high hills that runs from Ben Hope in Sutherland, by Ben Nevis to Ben Lomond. To the west of this line is an area of high rainfall (over 150 centimetres [60 inches] a year), while to the east is the drier hill country where heather moorland predominates. Behind the mountainous frontier of Drumalbyn, the sea-based Lordship of the Isles flourished and broke up, and the Campbells had a fastness from which they could expand.

GLEN NEVIS

A frosty morning in the glen, looking up towards Meall Cumhann. The precipitous slopes of Ben Nevis rise up out of sight to the left, until they reach the highest peak in Great Britain at 1,343 metres (4,406 feet).

GLEN ROY
The 'Parallel Roads' run along the sides of the glen at 350, 325 and 260 metres (1,150, 1,070 and 850 feet) above sea-level. Traditionally they were thought to be royal hunting roads, but since Louis Agassiz, the Swiss glaciologist, visited the glen in 1840, his suggestion that the 'roads' were the shorelines of former ice-dammed lakes has come to be accepted as correct.

The last of the ice ages ended only about 12,000 years ago. As the climate improved ice melted in hollows and created lochs and pools. Occasionally there were cataclysms, as in Glen Roy, when barriers of ice melted and whole lochs emptied their water into the surrounding countryside. Water flowed from the melting glaciers to make rivers.

In Greenland, the present-day retreat of the ice-cap provides us with examples of similar conditions to those found here 12,000 years ago. In Scotland then, as in Greenland now, the rivers were probably colonized at first by charr and sticklebacks only (in contemporary Greenland only one river has a natural salmon run). Then salmon, trout, and eels occupied the lochs and rivers. Eventually, the progeny of some of these colonizing species, brown trout, charr and powan, formed landlocked non-migratory populations, while those of others (salmon and eels) continued their migratory habits.

As the climate improved plants recolonized the ground. Short tundra gave way to grasslands and eventually to forest. First among the colonizing trees were the birches and willows with hazel. They were followed by Scots pine that, in due course, gave way to oak, ash and elm on the lower ground. Many forms of animal life, from invertebrates to birds and mammals, including reindeer, lynxes, brown bears, and beavers, immigrated as the vegetation began to support suitably sustaining habitats. The climatic peculiarities of the different parts of the Highlands started to make themselves felt. The West Highlands, up to a tree line that varied as the different climatic phases succeeded each other, developed a forest mainly of oak, although with some pine. The Eastern Highlands, earlier dominated by birch forest, were colonized by Scots pine that, with the birch, became the characteristic forest of that area. In the Northern Highlands, birch and willow with hazel woodland continued to dominate the country. Deterioration of the climate, resulting from increased rainfall and consequent soil acidification led to the formation of peat, making the pine less able to regenerate, and so more prone to suffer from the depredations of the post-glacial newcomer, man.

About 8,000 years ago, at much the same time as the great pine forests were developing, humans made their way into the Highlands. Some came by sea up the western coastline, perhaps in search of new fishing grounds, while others canoed in their dug-outs up eastern rivers such as the Tay. They used the rivers, the lochs and the shoreline because the dense forests and marshes of the interior were too daunting. As these hunter-gatherers settled territories and ranges, so they needed to exchange women, to trade axes and other artefacts, and to meet for religious purposes. They developed overland routes, many of which are still in use today, whether as motorways or footpaths. They also began to have an impact on their wider environment. Humans learned early that if you set fire to woodland, the flush of grasses and shrubs that initiates the process of vegetational recolonization encourages the wild game.

While the extent of the hunter-gatherers' activities can only be guessed at, the important thing about the shift to farming 4–5,000 years ago is that permanent changes started to be made to the countryside. Clearings were made in the forest, sometimes simply by grazing livestock, sometimes by ring-barking the trees and then burning them, and sometimes with the axe. Timber dwellings were built in the clearings, and the nearby ground could be cultivated. Livestock, initially mainly sheep and goats but also cattle and pigs, could be grazed further afield. It is in the Neolithic period that the great ritual landscapes of the Highlands began to develop, with the accumulation of burial sites and monuments in places such as Kilmartin in Argyll.

The Mesolithic hunters may have accelerated soil erosion by burning the forest to make clearings for hunting game, but what of the soils of the Highlands in general? Over much of the country, particularly in areas of high rainfall and where the underlying rocks are acidic, the soils are indeed poor, and wetter climatic phases have resulted in the growth and expansion of peat, but there are areas, such as Breadalbane and Atholl, where bands of limestone underlie large tracts of ground. In such areas, wherever the slopes are not too steep, or the rainfall too high, agriculture was practised on the brown forest soils that had developed there. In the Middle Ages the Lordship of the Isles' wealth was founded on the fertile soils of Islay; and the gentle climate and soils of Loch Awe-side and Glassary gave the Campbells their territorial base.

In about 600 BC the Iron Age reached the Highlands. The arrival of iron technology coincided with a deterioration in the climate, and

LOCH EILT
In a bare landscape this wooded island (probably planted) in Loch Eilt tells its own story: one patch of green safe from the threat of grazing or burning.

found an application in the making of weapons. Iron's readier availability caused it to replace bronze in their manufacture. The people of the high settlements faced starvation. They had to find somewhere else to live. In the mean time, those lower down, presented with an increasingly difficult climate themselves, had to defend their land and communities from the raiding of the occupants of the higher ground. From this time settlements had ramparts and ditches. These Celtic people emerge in history in about AD 300 as the Picts. Before that they had existed as several tribes, but the threat of Roman expansion probably brought them together into the confederations that reduced their political existence to two groups: the Northern Picts, with their capital at Inverness, probably at Craig Phadrig or Urquhart Castle; and the Southern Picts, whose main capital was near Perth.

Contacts between Ulster and Argyll existed from about AD 100 and Argyll's colonization by the Gaels of Dalriada in Ulster may have begun as early as the second or third century AD. They crossed the North Channel between Ireland and Scotland and by AD 500 had made the hill fort of Dunadd in Argyll their capital.

The rainy, cool period that had started perhaps as early as 1200 BC deteriorated from about 600 BC. It was followed from about AD 400 to 1200 by a recovery of the climate, characterized, particularly from AD 800, by relative freedom from storms in the Atlantic and the North Sea. In 793, the first Viking raid on Lindisfarne took place and, in 795, the first raid on Iona. A terrible storm had broken on the vulnerable coastal settlements of the British Isles and on the previously safe havens of the west. The initial shock of the Norse impact on Iona and the religious communities was devastating, made worse by the destruction of the library at Iona, one of the most important then existing in the Western world. Yet, within two centuries the Norse raider settlers had been converted to Christianity and their kings of the Western Isles were being buried alongside the Scots kings in the holy soil of Iona. The Norse and the Gael mixed and married, giving rise to the Gall-Ghaidheil—the Stranger-Gaels. The progenitors of some of the best known clans came from this stock. Clan Donald is descended from Donald, grandson of Somerled, a Gall-Ghaidheal. The MacLeods, also, claim descent from Leod, a chief of Norse ancestry.

BUICHAILLE ETIV MOR
'The Great Herdsman of Etive' (left) guards the entrance to Glencoe and to Glen Etive, famous for its associations with Deirdre of the Sorrows.

CRUACHAN FROM GLEN NANT
Cruachan Beann (right) is the talismanic hill of the Campbells. Its twin peaks give it the name of hipped one (cruach is the Gaelic for hip). 'Cruachan' was the war cry of the Campbells.

The Norse domination of the Western seaboard had important consequences for the development of Scotland. The relics of Saint Columba were moved from Iona to Dunkeld in about AD 805 and the pressure of the Norse raiders on the west coast contributed to the eventual union of the Picts and the Scots of Dalriada under Kenneth MacAlpin in about AD 843. Dunkeld, already a religious seat, became the capital of the new kingdom of Alba. The descendants of Kenneth MacAlpin went on to bring in the British (or Brythonic) state of Strathclyde, and then the Anglian kingdom of Lothian; but the geographical remoteness of the far north-west meant that they were unable to break the Norse domination of that area without some strengthening of their authority. The marriage of Malcolm III Canmore (*ceann mhór* means big head) to the English Margaret of Hungary in about 1070 marked a turning of the Scottish Court towards the south and towards new institutions, both in government and in the encouragement given to monastic orders to settle in Scotland.

RED DEER IN GLEN CASSLEY
In recent decades insufficient culling has led to a marked increase in the numbers of red deer. This has resulted in increased grazing pressure and so has jeopardized regeneration of native woodlands.

In the reigns following that of Malcolm III, especially in the times of David and William the Lion, knights, often the younger sons of Anglo-Norman families (among whom were included many men of Breton and Flemish descent), were encouraged to go to Scotland and settle there. Some found their way into the Highlands and contributed to the superimposition of ideas of feudalism on to existing ideas about land holding and the relations between chief and follower. Some of the most familiar Highland surnames today started as the names of Anglo-Norman adventurers in the early Middle Ages. They include Chisholm, Cummin, Fraser, Grant, Menzies, Murray, Stewart.

The tension between Norwegian rule of the Islands and the North-west and the ambitions of the Scottish Crown focused on the need for local rulers to swear allegiance to both authorities. Islands would be held from Norway and mainland ground would be held from the king of Scotland. In 1263 King Haakon sailed down the west coast exacting tribute and oaths of allegiance. In August of that year he was brought to battle at Largs. There was a storm at sea and the land battle was inconclusive, but Haakon's failure to win a decisive victory was a recognition that the Norwegian grip on its Scots dominions was no longer strong enough to withstand determined opposition. In 1266

Norway ceded the Western Isles to Scotland, a decisive moment in the country's history.

The loosening of the Norwegian grip on the Western Isles led to an opportunity for local leaders to dominate the area, above all in the Lordship of the Isles. The establishment of the Lordship coincided with, probably stimulated, a flowering of Gaelic art, of which the carved crosses and grave slabs at Kilmory and Keills in Knapdale, and the poetry in the *Book of the Dean of Lismore*, are examples. However, the attempts of the Lordship to gain the Earldom of Ross and the tendency to treat opportunistically with the kings of England contributed to the eventual suppression of the Lordship in 1493.

The period from 1490 to 1590 became known as the Linn nan Creach (the Age of the Forays) to the Gaels. The ending of the Lordship of the Isles under Clan Donald started the long fission of that clan and accelerated the rise of the Campbells. James IV delegated his responsibility and put the different parts of the Highlands under the authority of several great magnates.

Between about 1200 and 1400 the climate had worsened again with a period of partial recovery from 1400 to 1550. Then, in about 1550, there was another deterioration in the climate. This period of colder climate, known as 'The Little Ice Age' to climatologists, lasted until about 1750 and overlapped with the Age of the Forays, various later disturbances, and civil war. Apart from aggravating tensions (resulting, for example, from harvest failures) that led to warfare and raiding, the poor climate forced many Highlanders to seek employment as mercenary soldiers in Ireland during the sixteenth century and on the continent in the following century. From the late seventeenth century Highlanders started to seek seasonal work in the Lowlands, especially at harvest time. Recourse to this form of employment also followed the main expansion of the cattle trade from the late seventeenth and early eighteenth centuries and this was to play an important part in the Highland economy for the next two hundred years.

The 'discovery' of the Highlands by outsiders in the late sixteenth and early seventeenth centuries and the revelation that some large woods still existed there led to their exploitation, but not necessarily to their further destruction. The evidence of the early maps shows that the

RED SMIDDY
This is one of the iron foundries set up in the West Highlands in the early seventeenth century. English workers were brought to Wester Ross to make iron and cast cannon and some of their descendants were still living in the district in the late nineteenth century, recognizeable by their English surnames.

$\mathcal{L}$OCH LOMOND, THE TROSSACHS AND BALQUHIDDER

LOCH LOMOND, the Trossachs and Balquhidder have attracted visitors since the eighteenth century because of their scenery and, more recently, for their associations with Sir Walter Scott's 'The Lady of the Lake', William Wordsworth's 'Solitary Reaper' and Gerard Manley Hopkin's 'Inversnaid', which anticipates the message of environmental conservation. Rob Roy MacGregor was also born and active in this area.

Loch Lomond has the largest area of fresh water in the British Isles. It is of great scientific interest for its fish ecology (its waters hold populations of seventeen native species), for the fact that it straddles the Highland line and for the native oak woods that surround it. Close to the Glasgow conurbation, the area has known intense visitor pressure for as long as any other area in the world. This alone makes the failure to give it the protection it deserves as a national park all the more extraordinary.

The area is criss-crossed with old drove roads, most of which are still in use as main roads. The road along Loch Lomond itself (past the beach north of Tarbet where the MacGregors and the MacFarlanes exchanged ill-gotten cattle) leads through Glen Falloch with its remnant pine wood and the cave where, reputedly, Robert I hid and reflected on the spider. At Crianlarich this road, the A82, joins the A85 and follows the line of the old road that went east by the north shore of Loch Earn to Crieff, where the great cattle sales were held until their removal to Falkirk. On the east side of Loch Lomond is Inversnaid and the drove road that leads past Loch Katrine. This is the country of Rob Roy and it is immortalized in Dorothy Wordsworth's account of her visit there with her brother, William, in 1803.

LOCH LOMOND
Loch Lomond is the largest area of fresh water in the British Isles. A line of islands at the south end of the loch—from Inchmurrin, through Creich, Torrinch and Inniscailloch—marks the Highland boundary fault. From here south the loch is like a lowland lake.

ROWARDENNAN *(overleaf)*
The oakwoods of the Highlands formed part of the oak forest that, 7,000 years ago, stretched from the south-west of England through to Sutherland. Most surviving oakwoods, such as these at Rowardennan, are found on south-facing valleys and river sides.

THE MAKING OF THE CLANS

There is a map which shows the territories of clans and families throughout Scotland. The Colquhouns of Luss are positioned on the west side of Loch Lomond, more or less where they live today. The MacFarlanes are a little further north. On the east side, in Balquhidder, there are MacGregors, MacLarens and Stewarts and further south, in the Trossachs, are the Buchanans. To the north and west, in Argyll and Breadalbane, are the Campbells to whom, at one time or another, nearly all the smaller kindreds paid tribute. Straddling the Highland line, the Grahams ruled over their tenants and dependants.

The map is the well-known one prepared by the late Sir Iain Moncrieff of that Ilk and Don Pottinger, and represents the state of Scotland clan-wise in the early seventeenth century. It is a snapshot because territories and estates were continually changing, as was the nature of the clans themselves.

If we go back to our snapshot of the clans in 1600 we can imagine a clan in terms of a chief and his family. They occupied a territory, for which the chief had a charter from the Crown, or from a major aristocrat like Mac Cailein Mor, the chief of the Campbells. Men related to the chief occupied farms mainly in exchange for military service. These men were the *daoine uaisle* (the gentry), the officer class of the clan, and came to be called tacksmen from the seventeenth century onwards as the practice of granting them their land by written leases spread. Up until the early seventeenth century they were simply the *daoine uaisle* and held land by word of mouth from their chiefs. They sub-let their tenancies to family groups who did the farming. Below this group were landless cottars and others. In his own household a chief might have (depending on his wealth) a bard, a harper, a spokesman, a sword bearer, a piper, someone to carry him over streams and a gillie to lead his horse. The earls of Argyll had hereditary physicians, armourers and other functionaries. The chief's duties included providing land for his followers, settling disputes among them and supporting them in disputes with outsiders. The chief led a society characterized by feuding and feasting.

Within the territory of a powerful chief there might be other kin groups, not of the chief's clan, who had asked for his protection. Often

REMNANT PINES IN GLEN FALLOCH
Glen Falloch, near Crianlarich, is the south-western limit of the native pinewoods' range in the Highlands. Fences have been erected to exclude deer and grazing livestock and so help the process of natural regeneration.

these groups were absorbed into the clan of the chief whose ground they occupied, and sometimes they took on the name of the chief's family. It was important for a chief to have a good following because this was his power base.

James VI was determined to subjugate the clans. In 1609 he imposed the Statutes of Iona upon the Highland chiefs. They were to swear obedience to the King and there were to be restrictions on the number of followers each chief might have in his retinue and in his military following. Island chiefs were to be restricted in the numbers of galleys that they might own. Chiefs were to educate their sons in the Lowlands where they would learn English. King James's statutes marked an important symbolic point in the history of the Highlands because, although they did not change things immediately, they set out a prospect for change that was to be realized in due course. Surpluses of grain and cattle, whether got by the toil of the peasantry or by raiding, would no longer be so necessary for the maintenance of the feuding and feasting economy and the support of large numbers of followers. Eventually surpluses would be exported and then cattle would become more important than men.

FROM RAIDERS TO DROVERS

Cattle have been central to Celtic society since the Bronze Age. From medieval times it was recognized that the Highlands had considerable possibilities for grazing cattle, but it was not until the seventeenth century that their large-scale export became a major part of the economy.

If the harvest failed cattle were a source of income with which to buy food for the winter. They were also the prey of raiders from other parts of the country where the harvest had been unsuccessful. To prove himself a young chief was often expected to lead a raid into another clan's country, or into the Lowlands. Lifting cattle, then driving them home, often over great distances (perhaps from Strath Ardle in Perthshire over to Lochaber), and their eventual consumption or sale presented considerable problems. A clean lift and a successful return were a feat of leadership. The MacGregors and MacFarlanes on Loch Lomond-side had an arrangement whereby they exchanged cattle they had lifted so that when it came to disposing of the beasts they were sold in a market

INCHLONAIG ISLAND
Legend has it that this island in Loch Lomond was planted with yew at the command of King Robert I to provide longbows for the men of Lennox. Bows were in common use in the Highlands until the late seventeenth century.

EILEAN MOLACH, LOCH KATRINE
*Rob Roy was born in Glen Gyle
House at the head of Loch Katrine.
Eilean Molach, where Rob Roy
imprisoned Graham of Killearn, was
later immortalized by Sir Walter Scott
as 'Ellen's Isle' in his long narrative
poem 'The Lady of the Lake'.*

far from their home, and so would be less likely to be recognized. For those who lost their cattle the consequences could be serious. Without the means to buy grain in a season of famine they faced starvation.

Cattle raiding was not thought of as theft by the Highlanders, but as a legitimate activity, so long as it was carried out between clans rather than within them. It was one in which all the clans indulged at one time or other, but it was a particular necessity for groups like the MacGregors, the MacDonells of Keppoch and the MacDonalds of Glencoe, people with little or no arable ground of their own, or uncertain security of tenure, or both. The Breadalbane men, the Camerons and, further north, the MacKenzies were all considered to be notorious raiders of cattle in the early eighteenth century and this continued to be the case until the pacification of the Highlands later that century.

During the eighteenth century, when the cattle export trade was at its height, drovers would appear each autumn to buy cattle, even in the remotest districts. They would offer the sellers some cash and give out promissory notes for the rest of the value of the cattle. These notes passed quickly into circulation as currency, which enabled the farmers to pay their rent and to buy any necessary goods, such as grain, from the Lowlands.

From the middle of the eighteenth century the drover's lot became safer, but things were not at all easy during the seventeenth and early part of the eighteenth centuries. A drover might need to take the cattle he had bought, usually on someone else's behalf, over a great distance through the Highlands. It would be essential for him to pay protection money to the clans through whose land he was to travel, or to men like Rob Roy, who made a profession of arranging safe passage for drovers in exchange for payment.

Droves covered about ten miles a day and they would stop for the night at a stance, often near an inn, such as Kingshouse at the head of Glencoe, or Kingshouse at Balquhidder. As the eighteenth century wore on into the nineteenth century the customary stances, and even some of the old drove roads, became subject to the desire of landowners to enclose their land and so to deny the drovers' old rights of way.

Until the great expansion of the trade to provide beef for England and the Lowlands of Scotland, cattle were valued at least as much for

their dairy produce as for beef and hides. They were smaller than modern Highland cattle, although it is difficult to be precise about this because the values of weights have changed. Nowadays, we think of Highland cattle as being mainly a golden colour. This was not the case in earlier times. During the eighteenth century they were referred to as 'black cattle', but this seems to have been an exaggeration. There are many references in songs of that time to white-shouldered cattle, and a song attributed to Mary MacLeod, the seventeenth-century poetess, mentions the white-hoofed cattle of Ullinish in Skye.

The increase in the number of cattle through the eighteenth century had significant environmental consequences. Some of the deforestation that has been attributed to grazing by sheep from the late eighteenth century was almost certainly due to cattle, and to the goats that were then common in the Highlands.

ROB ROY, LAIRD OF INVERSNAID

Rob Roy MacGregor of Inversnaid (known officially all his life as Robert Campbell) is one of the most controversial figures of Highland history. Some see him as a Gaelic Robin Hood, while others as no more than a clever, common thief, and a brigand of no fixed loyalties.

Rob Roy MacGregor was born in February 1671 at Glengyle, the third son of Donald MacGregor of Glengyle, from whom he inherited Inversnaid. The MacGregors of Glengyle, known as Clann Dhubhghaill Chiar in Gaelic (Children of Dark Dougal) were descended from Donnchadh Ladasach (Lordly Duncan) MacGregor, who was beheaded at Balloch (now Taymouth Castle) at the east end of Loch Tay, in 1552.

Rob Roy's mother was born a Campbell of Glenlyon. She was the sister of Captain Robert Campbell of Glenlyon, who commanded the Government troops at the Massacre of Glencoe. The Campbell connection was important to Rob Roy and meant that he was able to look to his kinsman, the Earl of Breadalbane (Iain Glas 'Grey John'), the chief of the powerful Campbells of Glenorchy, for support in times of difficulty.

Living in the disturbed times of the late seventeenth and early eighteenth centuries, and coming from a clan which was still subject to the

THE CLADACH MOR
The chief of the MacFarlanes had a house here and the beach, by the side of Loch Lomond, was the meeting place for the exhange of ill-gotten cattle between the MacGregors and the MacFarlanes. No doubt as a result of these activities, the moon has long been known as MacFarlane's lantern in these parts.

ban on its existence imposed by James VI, Rob Roy lived the composite existence of de facto chief, farmer and cattle drover, protection racketeer, Highland Jacobite, soldier, and, some think, double agent. He was present at the Battle of Killiecrankie on 27 July 1689.

In 1691, he was involved in a cattle rustling incident at Kippen in Stirlingshire, which developed into an open battle between the villagers of Kippen and the MacGregors. The affair came to be known as the herriship (the plundering) of Kippen.

In 1712, Rob Roy's chief drover absconded with £1,000, which had been raised from the Duke of Montrose and a number of other gentlemen for the purchase of cattle. They did not give Rob Roy the chance to redeem the crime of his employee. His property at Craigroyston was forfeited, and the stock and furniture seized and sold. The way in which he was harassed by the Duke of Montrose ensured Rob Roy's enmity. He moved north to seek the protection of the Earl of Breadalbane and lived for a time in a cottage in Glendochart, from where he carried out a number of escapades.

Rob Roy was active in the Jacobite Rising of 1715. He was at Braemar for the raising of the Royal Standard on 6 September of that year, took part peripherally in the blundered Battle of Sheriffmuir, and was listed in the Act of Attainder for treason in 1717.

In November 1716 he carried out his most famous raid when he kidnapped the Duke of Montrose's factor, Graham of Killearn, along with 'what money he had got, his books, papers and bonds to a considerable value.' Graham was held on an island on Loch Katrine for two or three days before being restored to the Duke with all his papers but less the money—to the extent of about £1,000 sterling.

Pursuit became hot, and in the next three years Rob Roy was captured three times (once by the Duke of Atholl who imprisoned him at Logierait, by what is now the A9 south of Pitlochry). Each time he managed to escape.

He fought at the Battle of Glenshiel in 1719. In 1720 he settled in Balquhidder and was pardoned in 1725 through the good offices of General Wade, possibly in recognition of services rendered. He died peacefully in his bed in 1734 at Inverlochlarig on the northern shore of Loch Voil and is buried in the churchyard at Balquhidder.

ROB ROY'S GRAVE
After a life full of violent escapades, Rob Roy MacGregor died peacefully in his sleep in 1734, at the age of 62. He is buried in the churchyard at Balquhidder.

THE OAKWOODS OF ACHRAY (overleaf)
Two hundred years ago woods such as these above Aberfoyle were managed under a coppice system, a form of management widespread throughout the British Isles.

BARRACKS AT INVERSNAID
The barracks were built in 1718–19 to house 100 men as part of the measures to pacify the Highlands following the Jacobite Rising of 1715.

LANDSCAPE OF THE GAEL

The building of roads by the army, and the pacification of the country during the eighteenth century, brought visitors to the Highlands. Some, like William and Dorothy Wordsworth, Robert Burns, John Keats and a host of other poets, artists and literary figures came to look at the view. Others, like Dr Johnson and James Boswell, came to see a 'primitive state of society', but were too late. Others again were scientists, like James Hutton the geologist, and Thomas Pennant the naturalist. There were some who came to do something, like James Hogg the Ettrick shepherd, who came to farm, Thomas Telford the engineer, who came to make roads and canals, and Knox the philanthropist bookseller, who came to suggest fishery possibilities. Whatever else they were, they were outsiders. When the admirers of scenery among them looked about, as the Wordsworths did, they considered the way in which mountains were grouped together. They looked at woods and trees and stretches of water as scenery.

What of the Gaels themselves? They had no aesthetic concept of landscape to match that of the visitors. The land had a functional reality and necessity for the Highlanders, but their interaction with their country went much deeper. Not only did it bear the names of settlements and topographical features that themselves had deep meaning, as the frequent reference to places in songs shows, but the components of the landscape had symbolic importance. This went to the roots of Gaelic consciousness itself.

The letters of the Gaelic alphabet are each represented by trees or bushes. Thus *ailm*, the Gaelic for elm, stands for the letter A. B is represented by *beithe*, Gaelic for birch, and so on through the eighteen letters of the alphabet. The Celtic Calendar was also based on the trees of the alphabet. Each month was represented by a symbolic tree or bush. Birch was seen as the tree of beginning, which makes sense to any forester because it is such a splendid colonizing species. Hazel was the tree of an autumn month because its nuts ripen then. These two examples can only hint at the way in which the world view of the Gaels was bound up with their experience of the land as their physical support. This understanding of nature gave them a world that was to be experienced, a world in which function and belief were closely integrated.

LOCH ARKLETT
The loch drains into the Snaid Burn and so into Loch Lomond. The troubled genius Gerard Manley Hopkins composed his poem 'Inversnaid' after a visit here in 1881.

Much of our current awareness of the Gaelic landscape comes to us from the songs. We are made aware of the countryside by references to oak and hazel, the branchy woods, the hill sides, lochs and glens. There is frequent allusion to places. Often we may think that the mention of plants and trees has a simply naturalistic context-setting function, but we have to beware. Our own culture has lost the understanding of the frame of reference that gives certain allusions a particular significance.

The names of places printed on maps show that hills were given names that reflected certain characteristics: broad slopes, rocky sides, pointed peaks, likeness to the breasts of women. Sometimes they commemorated an event in history or myth. The Sgùrr nam Spainnteach in Kintail is a remembrance of the Spanish troops who fought alongside the Jacobite Highlanders in the Glenshiel Rising of 1719. The Sgor nam Fiannaidh in Glencoe gets its name from association with the Fenian band of the hero tales.

Baile- names indicate a farming township and names with *ach-* (from *achadh* meaning field) as prefixes often show where a secondary farming settlement developed when the population had outstripped the resources of the original township. The Christian past is recalled in the many *cill-* (meaning chapel) names. A glance over a map will show many references to different types of woodland, often where there are no woods now. The words *darach* or *doire* indicate the presence of oak woods, *giubhsach* means pine wood. *Feàrna* is the word for the alder tree and *call* or *calltuinn* means hazel.

The names of water courses indicate the size of the stream (*uisge*, a large river like the Spey; *abhainn*, a middle-sized river; *allt*, a stream or burn; *sruth*, a rushing rivulet) while the second part of the name may be simply descriptive, or have an ancient Pictish, pre-Indo-European element, whose meaning has been lost.

The entirety of this landscape, with its importance as the means of survival along with its familiarity as the community of the land, and the interweaving of these notions with the symbolic, the cultural and religious content of the Celtic world view, combined to produce the idea of *dùthchas*, the idea of heritage and hereditary right. This congregation of ideas is assembled in the word *dùthaich*, the more than motherland of the Gaels.

BEN MORE
Linked with Stobinian by a ridge, Ben More is a striking landmark from the west in Argyll and from Loch Tay in the east. It has been included in the proposed Natural Heritage Area.

$\mathscr{A}$THOLL AND BREADALBANE

BLAIR CASTLE
The home of the dukes of Atholl, the castle comprises a thirteenth-century tower (built by the ubiquitous Comyns to the annoyance of the earls of Atholl of the time) and many later alterations, including work carried out in the 1870s by David Bryce.

BREADALBANE IS BOUNDED by Rannoch to the north and Tyndrum to the west. Its eastern limit stretches beyond Kenmore. Atholl lies to the east and north of Breadalbane. Its limits in those directions are the pass of Drumochter, then round by the Forests of Dalnacardoch and Dalnamein, over to Glen Shee by the head of Glen Tilt (beyond which rise the high hills of the Cairngorms) and so down to the mouth of Strath Ardle, and across to Dunkeld.

From Breadalbane through much of Atholl and into parts of Glen Shee, bands of limestone and other base-rich rocks have given rise to some fertile soils. These rocks are a major factor in the development of the unusual Arctic/Alpine flora of Ben Lawers and the hills of Breadalbane. The good soils of the district are a reason why farmers, from Neolithic times on, have favoured this area, and why Atholl was a centre for the Southern Picts, and later a powerful earldom.

Breadalbane was one of the areas inhabited by the MacGregors, but the poem about them, written in 1604, on the death of the clan chief Alasdair of Glenstrae, has as its setting all the country between Loch Fyne and Strath Fillan. When the anonymous poet mentions the Srath na Dige she is speaking of the same country that Donnchadh Ban Macintyre was to describe 150 years later in his poignant *Cumha Coire Cheathaich* ('Lament for the Misty Corrie'). Donnchadh Ban nan Oran (Fair Duncan of the Songs) composed many poems on a wide range of subjects, one of which is in praise of the Black Watch. This regiment, the oldest Highland regiment in the British Army, was embodied on the banks of the River Tay at Aberfeldy in 1739.

Atholl and Breadalbane are today primarily stock-rearing country and many farmers in the area bear the old names—Campbell, MacDiarmid, MacNaughton, Robertson and Stewart—and are members of the pioneering lamb marketing co-operative, Highland Glen Producers.

THE FORTINGALL YEW
The ancient yew at Fortingall is thought to be the oldest tree in the British Isles. It is at least 2,000 and may be as much as 5,000 years old. The tree is thought have been associated with a sacral centre at which rulers were inaugurated in pre-Christian times and later Saint Adaman was active in the area. Today only a part of the ancient yew remains.

THE QUEEN'S VIEW *(overleaf)*
This view of Loch Tummel got its nickname in 1843, when Queen Victoria was brought here to admire it. The loch is now part of a hydro-electric scheme.

THE STONE AXE FACTORY OF BEINN NA CAILLICH

While he was carrying out a survey of the plant ecology of Breadalbane in 1954, Dr Duncan Poore passed by the foot of Beinn na Caillich (Hill of the Old Woman, or perhaps the witch or the white goddess), above Killin. He was looking for communities of Arctic/Alpine flowers at the foot of the rocky scree face of the hill when he noticed some small chippings of rock among the larger scree material and wondered if they might have resulted from human activity. He told archaeologists what he had seen and, in due course, a visit was made to the site. The eventual outcome of the archaeologists' investigation was a full-scale dig that revealed the remains of Scotland's only known mainland Neolithic axe factory. Since then analysis of the stone of which the axe heads were made has shown that axes from Killin have been recovered as far south as Buckinghamshire in southern England. The commonest origins of axes discovered in Scotland have been Rathlin Island off the coast of Northern Ireland, Tieve Bulliagh in Antrim, and the well-known axe factories of Cumbria in England. The distribution of stone axe heads is important evidence of our Neolithic ancestors' patterns of travelling and trading.

Agriculture and the clearance of forest were important new activities undertaken by our Neolithic forebears during a period of warmer and drier climate than now. Fieldwork carried out by archaeologists in North-east Perthshire has shown that arable farming was carried on up to a height of 460 metres (1,500 feet) above sea-level in Strath Ardle and the Forest of Alyth from about 4,000 years ago. Some of the clearance of the woodland that covered the hill slopes then may have been done using the stone axes brought in by trade from Killin and further afield. It seems that the late-Neolithic to early Bronze-Age population of the Uplands, on the edge of the Grampian Highlands and extending along the sides of the glens and straths, was as large then as it has ever been.

SHIELINGS AND A SONG

If you study almost any map of the Highlands you are sure to notice names with the prefix *airigh* in the west, and *ruigh* in the east. Often these prefixes have been corrupted so you find that *airigh* becomes *ari* and *ruigh* becomes *ri*. These are Gaelic words for 'shieling', a word

LOCH RANNOCH
One of the lochs that radiates out from Rannoch Moor, it has on its north side the south-facing slope of the Slios Min *(Smooth Slope), valuable for its grazing and once the property of the Menzies. The loch itself is the home of a population of the Arctic charr and ferox trout.*

which means a summer grazing. The Ordnance Survey's 1:50,000, and better still 1:25,000, maps show the sites of shieling huts, such as those near the National Trust for Scotland's visitor centre at Ben Lawers near Loch Tay, and further over on the grassy southern face of the hill.

The ruined remains of shieling huts are to be found all over the Highlands and are a reminder of the system of transhumance that prevailed here, and in all the upland areas of Scotland, at various times in the past, and in some of the rest of the world to this day. They were occupied through the summer months by people who herded the cattle, sheep and goats on the high grazings.

In the autumn, after the harvest, the cattle, sheep and goats were brought back to the lower ground to eat any grain or grass that remained in the stubbles, and at the onset of winter those that had not been slaughtered or sold were housed. In spring, the livestock were driven out of the arable area of the settlement to graze on the low-ground pasture nearby. Before the stock left the low ground, an advance party went up to the shielings to prepare the huts for the summer. Then, some weeks later in early June, the main herds and flocks were driven up. This was an event of great excitement. Most of the men and the older women were left behind to repair dry stone walls, finish the cultivations, re-thatch the houses and so forth, and in due course, to bring in the harvest of bere (a kind of barley) and oats.

Up at the shielings the stock were herded and the women milked the sheep, cows and goats. Cheese, often an important part of the rent, was made, as was butter.

This was the time of the year for the young to enjoy themselves in the freedom of the hills. Girls were often left by themselves at the shieling huts and many songs tell of the visits of their sweethearts.

In the autumn, the livestock were driven down from the hill grazings, some of the cattle to be sold and driven away by the drovers for fattening in the pastures of lowland Scotland and England before slaughter the following year.

The end of transhumance in the Highlands happened gradually, sometimes with the lower shielings becoming permanent settlements at times of population growth. Otherwise the system came to an end when the summer grazing was detached from a family's farm as a result

THE BLACK WOOD OF RANNOCH
A fallen pine reveals its root system, a reminder that much of the biological diversity of the northern forests lies in the fauna and flora of their soils, whereas the diversity of the tropical forests is above ground. In the background are the tree trunks of the ancient wood.

of a landowner accepting a lowland grazier's bid for the area of the former summer pasture, or the conversion of the ground into deer forest.
These things happened increasingly throughout the eighteenth and
nineteenth centuries, but remnants of the old practice survived in the
Outer Isles into this century.

THE MACGREGORS

The story of the MacGregors is one of loss and eventually of survival.
Before the Campbells became the dominant force in Argyll, the Mac-
Gregors had held land in Glenorchy, including Glenstrae, and Glenlyon. Their chiefs were patrons of the arts and poems were dedicated to
them. From 1512 to 1526, James, a MacGregor of Roro in Glenlyon,
who had become Dean of Lismore, and his brother, Duncan, gathered
together the great collection of Gaelic poetry called the *Book of the
Dean of Lismore*. How was it that a family of this distinction should
give their name to a people who became a byword for lawlessness, and
one of whose branches should even come to be known as 'the Children
of the Mist'?

The key lies in their landlessness. In the fourteenth century, the Mac-
Gregors lost their right by charter to their lands in Glenstrae to the
Campbells and so eventually found themselves dispersed through
Argyll, Breadalbane, Rannoch and Glenlyon. Some settled as far away
as Deeside in Aberdeenshire. In the end, their violent protests against
the destruction of a way of life brought about an attempt to destroy
them forever.

There was much celebration in the autumn of 1589 on the safe
return home of James VI with his bride, Princess Anne of Denmark.
Instructions were given to the royal foresters to kill deer for the feasts
that were to take place at the Royal Court in Stirling Castle to celebrate
the marriage.

The hereditary forester in Glenartney, the nearest royal deer forest to
Stirling, was Patrick, Lord Drummond, and John Drummond of
Drummondernoch was one of his assistants. The order for venison for
the royal marriage festivities was enormous and one can imagine John
Drummond spying the land to see where the deer were grazing. He
went out on his own and was caught by a band of MacGregors from

MACGREGOR GRAVESTONES
*MacGregor chiefs lie in the Clachan
an Disiert (Dalmally), near the clan's
heartland of Glenorchy and
Glenstrae; land that was lost to them
when a MacGregor heiress married
a Campbell.*

Balquhidder, whose kin he had hanged for poaching in the Royal Forest some time before. They killed and beheaded him. Then, high on their vengeance, but perhaps already dismayed at the prospect of trouble, they started for home. They climbed over the shoulder of Ben Vorlich and made their way down to Ardvorlich, a stronghold of the Stewarts, where they found the laird's wife in, alone, and evidently pregnant. Perhaps they knew that Stewart of Ardvorlich's wife was the sister of Drummond, perhaps not, but they played a callous trick on her. They demanded food, which, by the rules of hospitality she was obliged to give. In any case what could she do, on her own, facing a band of armed men? She led them into the hall and gave them some bread. The story goes that she left the room to look for more food and, when she returned, she found, to her horror, the head of her brother on the table with a piece of bread stuffed into its mouth. Instantly she fled from the house and ran to a lochan not far from the summit of Ben Vorlich, where some weeks later she gave birth. She is said never to have regained her sanity, and the lochan is known to this day as Lochan na Mna (the Lochan of the Woman).

King James was furious when he heard what had befallen his forester and outlawed the whole of Clan Gregor. The chief, young Alasdair of Glenstrae, son of Gregor Ruadh, instead of repudiating the brutal action of his clansmen in Balquhidder, observed the ancient customary duty of a chief to back his men. He met them there in the churchyard and, with the head of the slain Drummond on a gravestone, swore that the clan would stand together. Their crime was his.

In spite of the decree of outlawry, the MacGregors managed to stave off disaster and then in December 1602 they carried out a spectacular raid on Colquhoun territory in Glenfinlas, a reprisal for the hanging of two MacGregors. They plundered forty-five houses, carried off 300 cattle, 400 sheep, 400 goats, and 100 horses. Two of the Colquhouns were killed.

Sir Humphrey Colquhoun of Luss was advised to make an issue of this outrage. It was well known that the King could not stand the sight of blood so it was suggested that he should stage a demonstration before the King with as 'mony bluidie sarks as ather are deid or hurt of zour men togither with als mony women'. As expected, James was

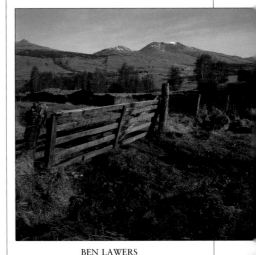

BEN LAWERS
Ben Lawers is famous for the richness of its Arctic/Alpine flora. The southern slopes are peppered with the remains of shieling huts, some of which are near the National Trust for Scotland's visitor centre. In the distance is Loch Tay, which has Taymouth Castle, once the seat of the Campbells of Breadalbane, at its east end. The River Tay, the largest river in the British Isles, flows out of the loch past the castle.

revolted by the sight of the shirts and the wailing of the women, and granted Sir Humphrey a commission against the MacGregors.

News reached the MacGregors of the Colquhouns' intentions and preparations, and Alasdair of Glenstrae decided to strike first. The MacGregors marched with stealth from Rannoch and Balquhidder, crossed Loch Lomond, and, catching the Colquhouns by surprise, routed them in Glenfruin, on 7 February 1603.

King James was incensed and developed a pathological and genocidal obsession against the MacGregors. Two days before he left for England an act of the Privy Council proscribed the name of MacGregor forever and laid down penalties for anyone who sheltered them. The Earl of Argyll, who had up to then stayed his hand against the MacGregors (having made use of them from time to time as mercenaries), saw that he would gain much from the King by persecuting the clan.

Alasdair of Glenstrae, chief of the MacGregors was caught by a deception and hanged in Edinburgh on 20 January 1604. In his speech from the gallows he made certain accusations against Argyll. One of these was that the Earl had betrayed the MacGregors in return for a grant of the lands of Kintyre, up till then belonging to Clan Donald. Archibald the Grim (Gilleasbuig Gruamach) of Argyll was, Alasdair claimed, buying MacDonald land with MacGregor lives. On 7 August 1607 the lordship of Kintyre was granted to the Earl of Argyll.

The persecution of the MacGregors is one of many tragic episodes of Scottish history. Yet they survived, finding refuge with kinsfolk in other clans and adopting their names. They became Campbells, Stewarts, Murrays, Drummonds, or they adapted their name to Gregory, or Greig if they went to live in the Lowlands. In 1644 they were back fighting under Montrose and Alasdair MacColla, for the King (the son of James VI and I who had tried to destroy them). In every rising from 1689 to 1745 Clan Gregor fought for the Stuarts in the hope of preserving Gaeldom from the threats of the changing times. The ban on the name was lifted finally in 1774.

THE RAISING OF THE BLACK WATCH

The departure of the army of occupation from the Highlands, after the Restoration of the Monarchy in 1660, was followed by a return to the

GLEN LYON
This view is towards Ruaro, with the River Lyon running between the Bridge of Balgie and Invervar. The glen was once famous as an area of MacGregor settlement and Campbell infiltration and possession. The Clann an sgeulaiche *(children of the storyteller), an offshoot of the MacGregors of Ruaro, were a musical and literary dynasty. They were the MacCrimmons of the Central Highlands and had a piping school at Drumcharry, east of Fortingall.*

RANNOCH MOOR
During the last ice age, around 14,000 years ago, the moor was the centre of a massive ice sheet that flowed out through the troughs that radiate from it—Loch Leven, Glencoe, Loch Etive, Loch Awe, Glenlyon, Loch Rannoch and Loch Treig. In more recent times it became a no-man's land of more than 250 square kilometres (100 square miles) divided between Lochaber, Argyll and Perthshire. It was the haunt of 'broken men' such as the members of Clan Gregor and served as summer grazing ground for the clans who lived on its borders.

less settled conditions that had preceded the rule of Cromwell. An impoverished central government was not prepared to pay for regular soldiers to garrison the Highlands. Several nobles and chiefs were commissioned to raise independent companies of gendarmes to police their areas. These companies survived the civil war between 1689 and 1692 and continued in existence until 1717, when only three remained and these were disbanded.

These independent companies had not fulfilled expectations. Cattle raiding continued as before. In the 1720s General Wade was to allege that the commanders of the independent Highland companies were almost without exception incompetent and corrupt.

In 1724, however, Lord Lovat, chief of the Highland Frasers, wrote a memorandum to the Government suggesting that independent companies should be raised again. The Government's response was to send General Wade, an internal security specialist, to the Highlands. His report recommended that six companies should be raised, and forts built or strengthened at various sites. A Spanish invasion scare in 1727 caused the strength of the companies to be increased further.

In their capacity as gendarmes, the independent companies had become known as Am Freiceadan Dubh (the Black Watch)—'Black' to distinguish them in their dark tartan kilts from the Government's regular infantry battalions who wore red coats, and 'Watch' because of their role as a watch against insurrection and the protection racket.

In 1739 the number of companies was raised to ten, and the following year they were embodied as the 43rd Regiment of Foot beside the River Tay at Aberfeldy. At this point the Highlanders, in the main solely Gaelic speakers, understood that the regiment was for home service only. However, faced with a shortage of manpower for its campaign in Flanders, the Government decided to draft the Black Watch there in 1743, and so deceived the soldiers. This resulted in a mutiny, the immediate outcome of which was its suppression and the shooting in the Tower of London of the three leaders. 108 of the 120 soldiers who had been actively involved were sent to the West Indies and the bulk of the regiment was persuaded that their future lay in the service of the British Government. They embarked for Flanders in May 1743 and stayed there until 1745. Then, as later, the British Government was cynical in its use of the Highlanders. It saw the Gaels as a source of manpower and small matter if they fell. In removing the Black Watch from the Highlands the Government made the mistake of stripping the country of a stabilizing military presence. This encouraged the Jacobites to rise, which they probably would not have done if the regiment had been at home.

At all events, the Black Watch served in the Flanders campaign and were restored to high morale by their fine commanding officer, Sir Robert Munro of Foulis. In 1745 the regiment covered the retreat of the British army at the Battle of Fontenoy with great heroism.

The exceptional performance of the Black Watch led to the raising of other Highland regiments and, in due course, to the rehabilitation of the Gaels in the eyes of the English and Lowland Scots. They were renumbered the 42nd Regiment of Foot in 1749.

BLACK WATCH MEMORIAL
The statue of the Black Watch soldier is by Rhynd, the late Victorian sculptor. Tay bridge, in the background, was designed by William Adam, father of the more famous Robert. It was built in 1733 by soldiers under the command of General George Wade, Commander-in-Chief in Scotland between 1725 and 1740, who had been charged with a project to construct a network of roads throughout the Highlands.

LORNE, MID-ARGYLL AND APPIN

LOCH AWE

This view looks along the north shore of the loch towards the Pass of Brander, where King Robert and his friends, the Campbells, defeated the MacDougalls in 1308. Today the loch is still dotted with crannogs—artificial islands—whose Bronze Age inhabitants worked the neighbouring arable land before retiring to their fastnesses at night. Crannogs remained in use up until the seventeenth century.

HUMANS HAD SETTLED in Argyll long before the Gaels from Ulster made it their home. Some of the earliest evidence of human occupation in Scotland (from Mesolithic times—10–7,000 years ago) has been found in the bay of Oban and on the shores of the islands of Jura and Oronsay. The landscape of mid-Argyll is rich in the monuments of peoples from Neolithic times on. However, it is the impact of the Gaels at the beginning of historical times and their contribution to the creation of modern Scotland that seems outstanding to us now. It was from Argyll that the Gaels expanded to found the Kingdom of Alba (and so Scotland) under Kenneth MacAlpin in AD 843. It was from this area, too, that much of the conversion to Christianity of Scotland north of the Forth took place, powered by the spiritual energy that emanated from the Abbey of Iona.

The Campbells settled in Lorne and flourished making some of the most significant contributions to the development of modern Scotland of any kindred, Highland or Lowland.

The coast of Argyll is said to be 1,000 miles long. It runs from Cowal in the south, by Kintyre through Knapdale, up Lorne to Appin, and on to those conquests of the Campbells, Morvern and Ardnamurchan. The shoreline is a mysterious land of oak woods, inlets and islands. Travelling up the road from Ardfern to Oban, Jura (Island of Deer) lies out to the west, with the famous whirlpool of Corrievreckan between it and Scarba (where the poetess, Mairi nighean Alasdair Ruaidh—Mary MacLeod—was exiled). From Oban, sea port for the islands, one can see Kerrera (where Alexander II died). Inland there are the lochs and roads that cut through the hills; the passes that lead the traveller out of Argyll.

Loch Awe, with its foot near Kilmartin and its head guarded by Kilchurn Castle, leads through to Breadalbane, on whose hills roamed

CLACH A'CHARRA, ONICH
The Clach a'Charra stands on the shores of Loch Linnhe. Many standing stones marked boundaries between divisions of land and some may have been memorials, gravestones, or have had an astronomical or calendrical function. This one may also have been a betrothal stone.

the poet Donnchadh Ban Macintyre. Between Loch Awe and Loch Etive, on the lower slopes of Ben Cruachan, is the Pass of Brander, where Robert I put the MacDougalls to flight.

Appin is famous for its Stewarts and, as motorists sweep over the bridge at Ballachulish on the way to Fort William, it is easy for them to overlook the monument to James Stewart, Seumas a'Ghlinne (James of the Glen) who was hanged nearby for the killing of Colin Campbell of Glenure in 1752. Going east from Ballachulish along the side of Loch Leven one passes Eilean Munde, burial ground of the MacDonalds of Glencoe. Then Glencoe itself rises ahead (its north-west end marked by the beautiful Sgùrr na Ciche or Pap of Glencoe), empty of MacDonalds but full of climbers.

DALRIADA AND DUNADD

The withdrawal of the Romans from Britain in AD 410 started a process of territorial reshuffling among the tribal Britons, the consequences of which were soon felt in Scotland. The arrival of the first expeditions of Dalriadans from Ulster may have started around AD 400, or even before, but it was not until about AD 500 that Fergus Mac Eirc landed in Scotland with two sons and about 150 men.

Fergus settled in Knapdale and Kintyre, and adopted the site of the existing fort at Dunadd as his home and the capital for all the Scots of Dalriada. Of his two sons, Angus settled on the island of Islay, and Loarn in the country which now bears his name, with his base at the fort of Dunolly, outside present-day Oban. The land that the two colonized became known as Oirer Gaidheal which means The Shoreline of the Gaels and survives as the name Argyll.

The Dalriadans were great seafarers and their choice of Dunadd was a good one. Three sea lochs, Gilp, Sween and Crinan reach in towards it, all with safe anchorages for vessels of shallow draft. The foot of Loch Awe, a little to the north of Kilmichael Glassary, is not far away, and from there quick access could be had to the interior of the country, via Dalmally and Breadalbane, so long as one's relations with the inhabitants of the many crannogs that dot that loch were amicable. The site of Dunadd was also a wise one because the fort commands a wide stretch of country. From the top of the dun an army could be seen two

CASTLE STALKER
Standing on the edge of Loch Linnhe, Castle Stalker was first built in the mid-sixteenth century. The tower was a stronghold of the Stewarts of Appin, a place of defence against unruly neighbours such as the MacDonalds of Glencoe. After lying ruined for over 200 years, the castle was restored during the 1960s.

THE FALLS OF ORCHY
The River Orchy tumbles through the Falls on its way to Loch Awe. A crude salmon ladder has been blasted from the rock to enable fish to reach spawning grounds further upstream.

or three miles away. It is interesting that the evidence of the pollen record suggests that the first extensive deforestation in Knapdale happened about 1,500 years ago, which was roughly the date of the establishment of Dalriada.

THE CAMPBELLS

It can truly be said of the Campbells, the castle of whose chief, the Duke of Argyll, is at Inveraray, that their origins are lost in the mists of antiquity.

During the Middle Ages, the kings and the nobility of Scotland rejected their Celtic past and, in a desire for respectability, Gaelic noble houses sought a genealogy which included, if it did not begin with, a Norman element. In the case of the Campbells it was judged suitable, probably during the sixteenth century, to add the 'p' to the name and insert a rather improbable Norman addition to the genealogy. This was accepted by many as correct until quite recently when David Sellar, the distinguished genealogist, showed that a British origin in the ancient kingdom of Strathclyde was more likely.

The first mention of them in Argyll is in the thirteenth century, by which time they had settled in Craignish and Kilmartin. There they found a number of other families, the MacSweens of Castle Sween, the Lamonts of Ardlamont, and the MacLachlans of Castle Lachlan in Strathlachlan. Other families with whom they had to compete for territory included the MacGilchrists and the MacNaughtons, lords of the castle of Innishail in Loch Awe.

By the end of the thirteenth century they had reached the north end of Loch Awe, and it was then that they had their big break. David Sellar has suggested a relationship between Robert Bruce's mother's family, that of the Earls of Carrick, and the Campbells. This is a possible reason for their alliance with Robert I in the Wars of Independence. At the time when Robert was on the run from the forces of Edward I of England, he could not have survived at all without the help of his great ally and friend, Sir Neil Campbell, and his son Sir Colin. At any event, when the war came to an end King Robert rewarded his Campbell allies generously at the expense of those who had fought against him. These included families like the MacDougalls, previously the most

BONAWE IRON FOUNDRY
*This foundry was established in 1753
by Cumbrian iron masters. James
Watt (of steam engine fame) thought
that the efforts to keep it supplied
with charcoal would destroy the
forests in the surrounding
countryside. Nowadays, however, it
is accepted that the woods exploited
by the eighteenth-century iron
masters owe their survival to this
industrial use. The foundry was
closed in 1876.*

powerful family of the region, the Macnabs (to whom the MacGregors were probably related), the MacSweens, the Lamonts and the Mac-Naughtons. These families were all allied with the Comyns, Lords of Badenoch, and took their side during that family's feud with King Robert following the King's murder of the Red Comyn at Dumfries on 10 February 1306.

The subsequent history of the Campbells until the nineteenth century was one of expansion. From the time of Sir Colin Campbell, friend of Robert I, the family was generally a supporter of the Crown. Throughout the fourteenth century it consolidated its territorial base in Argyll, and became important enough for its leader, the by then Earl of Argyll, to be appointed Lieutenant of the Isles after the forfeiture of the Lordship of the Isles by Clan Donald in 1493. During the sixteenth century the junior branch of Campbell of Breadalbane started on its expansion east to Perthshire, to settle eventually at Taymouth, at the eastern end of Loch Tay. Also in that century a Campbell married the heiress of the estate of Cawdor in Moray. Land in Angus was acquired by a Campbell abbot of Coupar Angus and, following the Reformation, handed on to his descendants.

After the Chaseabout Raid of 1565 in Queen Mary's reign, the temporarily victorious forces of the Crown did not pursue the Earl of Argyll. The reason for this apparent leniency was clear enough; the military and naval forces of the Earl were at least as great as those of the Crown. During the seventeenth century the Campbells acquired Ardnamurchan after destroying the chiefly family of the MacIains of Ardnamurchan, a branch of Clan Donald. Next they acquired Kintyre, heartland of the old Lordship of the Isles, and the island of Islay. They subjugated the MacLeans in Mull, Morvern and Tiree after taking on the debts of the MacLean chiefs in the 1670s.

The family faltered twice in the seventeenth century. On 2 February 1645, a terrible vengeance was taken upon them at the Battle of Inverlochy, following a violent winter when Royalist forces ravaged Argyll. Then, in 1685, the ninth earl sided with Monmouth in the brief rebellion which that unfortunate man raised against James VII and II. The Marquess of Atholl was made Lieutenant of Argyll and invaded Argyll in 1685 with a force of Athollmen and some other old enemies of the

THE RIVER ORCHY
The River Orchy flows into Loch Awe, at twenty-four miles, the longest freshwater loch in Scotland. Until the late fourteenth century Glenorchy and the neighbouring Glenstrae belonged to the MacGregor family. However they lost their title to the land when an heiress married one of the Campbells of Loch Awe.

Campbells, including the MacDonalds of Glencoe, and laid waste the country. They had instructions to exterminate the rebels and send the women and children into transportation. In spite of this unfortunate incident, or perhaps because of it (the Duke of Argyll was able to exact massive reparations from the newly-elevated Duke of Atholl), the Campbells were able to consolidate their position during the eighteenth century as upholders of the Protestant religion and of the Crown. That century saw the Dukes of Argyll as the most powerful magnates in the Highlands, and possibly in all Scotland.

THE MASSACRE OF GLENCOE

The Highland War of 1689 made it necessary for the Government to commit a number of infantry battalions and regiments of cavalry to Scotland. So far as King William was concerned this was a serious nuisance because he needed them in Flanders, where he was also busy making war. The Treaty of Achallader on 30 June 1691 brought the military campaign in the Highlands, which had started some months before the Battle of Killiecrankie, to an end, and the royal proclamation of 29 August of that year, requiring an oath of allegiance from the chiefs and their principal tenants by 1 January 1692, seemed to be taking the pacification of the Highlands a step further.

Some of the chiefs, however, still felt bound by their oaths of allegiance to King James, and said that they would need time to gain permission to be freed from that oath. King James delayed and did not release the chiefs from their oaths of allegiance to him until December 1691 and it took time for the news to reach the Highlands.

The Government decided that if the Highland chiefs would not agree to peace with King William an example would have to be made of a clan in order to ensure peace and order. The MacDonalds of Glencoe, notorious cattle reivers, were chosen largely because they were few, unpopular, and geographically exposed. Glencoe, with its precipitous sides, was the perfect trap.

The massacre became inevitable when Alasdair, the elderly chief of the MacDonalds of Glencoe, went to Fort William to swear his oath of allegiance to King William, when he should have gone to Inveraray, to swear it before the Sheriff of Argyll, Campbell of Ardkinglass. There

THE STONE CIRCLES OF TEMPLEWOOD
Situated near Kilmartin, these circles were discovered, along with a line of cairns with their burial chambers (all of the second and third millennia BC), in the early nineteenth century, when the valley was drained and peat skimmed off from the surface to lay bare the mineral (and so cultivable) soil beneath. The nearest stone has a spiral pecked out.

GLENCOE
Seen here from Loch Leven, the Sgorr na Ciche slopes up to the left. Behind, occupying the middle of the photograph, are Aonach Dubh and Stob Coire nan Lochan. The infamous massacre of the MacDonalds mainly took place further down in the delta of the glen.

followed the long snowy journey from Fort William by Kinlochleven and Ballachulish, detention overnight at Barcaldine and, finally, arrival at Inveraray on 2 January only to find that Campbell of Ardkinglass was at home on the other side of Loch Fyne, celebrating the New Year. The Sheriff returned to Inveraray on the fifth and accepted MacDonald's oath, but had to say that as it was late the oath was technically invalid. The old chief wept when he heard this, for he knew that he had played into the hands of his enemies. Sure enough, Sir John Dalrymple, Master of Stair, and the Privy Council in Edinburgh, with the connivance of Livingstone, Commander-in-Chief of the army in Scotland, and King William in London set in motion the machinery of state terror.

The soldiers of Argyll's regiment, most of whom were not Campbells, arrived in Glencoe on 1 February, and were billeted among the MacDonalds. This was a standard way of collecting arrears of tax in kind and so aroused no suspicion among the people of the glen. As they ate and drank with the MacDonalds and took part in the life of the glen, it is not surprising that some of the soldiers became friendly with their hosts, and so when orders were given to massacre the MacDonalds on the night of the twelfth, hints were made, and indeed Campbell of Glenlyon, the commanding officer, failed to set guards on the southern passes of the glen. At five o'clock on the morning of 13 February the killing began. About a dozen people died in the massacre, including the old chief and his family, and another couple of dozen died of exposure out on the hill side, but most of the clan escaped.

The massacre was a small one in the history of human barbarity, and in mid-seventeenth-century Scotland it would hardly have rated a footnote in the annals. However it earned considerable notoriety, partly because of the traditionally heinous nature of 'murder under trust', and partly because slaughter by the State and the conspiracy that had achieved it seemed particularly disgraceful. The Jacobites were later able to make much of this example of perfidious behaviour by the new king towards his people.

It might be said that the massacre achieved its aim in one respect. There was peace in the Highlands and King William was able to pursue his continental war.

INVERARY

Inverary was the capital of the Campbell's Argyll and the site of the Duke's castle, courthouse and gaol (now a museum).

LOCH TULLA

The Blackmount Forest on the edge of Rannoch has a remnant of pinewood by the southern shores of Loch Tulla. Duncan Ban MacIntyre, poet and hunter of deer was born at Druimliaghart, not far from the loch. His poem 'Moladh Beinn Dobhrain' (In Praise of Ben Doran) has been described by another poet, Iain Crichton Smith, as the finest nature poem in any British language.

$\mathcal{L}$OCHABER

THE MAMORE HILLS
*Sunset over the hills of Lochaber.
Domhnall MacFhionnlaidh nan Dan,
the poet, roamed this area in
his career as MacDonald of
Keppoch's hunter.*

LOCHABER IS BOUNDED by Badenoch to the north-east, and by Moidart and Morvern to the north and west. To the south its limits are Loch Leven and Glencoe; to the east, Corrour. In the past the area was notorious for the activities of its cattle-lifting clans, the Camerons and their affiliates, and the MacDonells of Keppoch. The latter are also memorable for the number of poets they produced, most famously Domhnall MacFhionnlaidh nan Dan, Iain Lom MacDonald and Sileas na Ceapaich.

Brae Lochaber (Fort William through to Glen Spean) includes Glen Roy, famous as the route by which the army of Montrose and Mac-Colla Chiotaich approached Inverlochy in February 1645. Nearby is Mulroy, the site of the last clan battle (1688), where the MacDonells of Keppoch, reinforced by the Camerons, defeated the Macintoshes, who were supported by Government troops. Inverlair House, a few hundred yards away from Cillechoiril, the spiritual centre of Brae Lochaber, was the site of the Keppoch murder.

The Viscount of Dundee raised the Royalist forces at Mucomir near the foot of Loch Lochy before the campaign of 1689 that culminated in the Battle of Killiecrankie. There they defeated the Government army, commanded by General MacKay.

Fort William (originally a military garrison) lies on the shores of Loch Linnhe in the shadow of Ben Nevis, the highest mountain in the British Isles (1,343 metres [4,406 feet]), and on the slopes of the nearby Aonach Mor are the newest ski slopes in the Highlands. On the other side of Loch Linnhe, steam seeps from the orifices of the pulp mill at Corpach. Further down the Loch on the Ardgour side is the super quarry at Glen Sanda.

THE CAMERONS

The Camerons are of Gaelic origin. John Ochtery came into Lochaber as bailie of John, first Lord of the Isles. Either he or one of his

GLEN ROY
Bracken covers a hillside in Glen Roy. An aggressive fern, bracken invades ground that has been burnt too often. In the Highlands it has played a part in curtailing the natural regeneration of oakwoods.

descendants had a crooked nose, hence the nickname *Cam shron* which means crooked nose—a name which stuck. In 1429 Domhnall Dubh Cameron, descendant of John Ochtery, broke away from vassalage to the Lord of the Isles.

Having acquired land in Lochaber the Camerons started on a course of annexation and suppression. Some local kindreds, seeing the rise of the Camerons must have decided to acknowledge their importance and to accept their dominion. Others may have thought that they could resist, and so found themselves having to submit after the use of force. In this way, and by marriage, the Camerons absorbed such groups as the MacMartins, the MacSorleys of Glen Nevis, the MacGillonies, some MacPhees, the MacMasters and the MacMillans of Murlaggan by the side of Loch Arkaig.

The break-up of the Lordship in the fifty years that followed the forfeiture in 1493 gave clans like the Camerons the opportunity to develop within the area of the old Lordship. In 1528 James V granted the lands of Loch Arkaig and Glen Loy to Ewen, son of the famous chief, Alan of the Forays (Ailean nan Creach). Ewen was the first chief to be designated 'of Locheil'.

By the seventeenth century the Camerons were recognized by the Campbells as a buffer group between themselves and the Macintoshes to the north-east.

Although the Locheil of the time was a spectator at the Battle of Inverlochy in 1645 (from the vantage point of the Earl of Argyll's galley in Loch Linnhe, where he is said to have acted as a fifth column by exercising his reputation as a seer and prophesying Argyll's defeat), about 3–400 Camerons took part in the battle, fighting in the van of MacColla and Montrose's army.

The Cromwellian invasion of 1650 saw them joining the resistance to the English. However recognition of the Cromwellian conquest and the establishment of the new fort (later named Fort William), a little to the west of the old castle at Inverlochy, gave the Camerons an opening of an unexpected kind. The pragmatic Ewen Cameron of Locheil, having shown his warrior skills by biting out the throat of an English officer with whom he was engaged in single combat, won the contract to supply the garrison with vegetables and other victuals. Moreover, he

COMMANDO MEMORIAL
A tribute to the commandos who trained at Achnacarry during the Second World War.

arranged with the authorities that those of the name of Cameron might continue to bear arms. All other Highlanders had been forbidden to carry weapons, so this added to Cameron prestige.

The Restoration of the Monarchy in 1660 was, for a moment, embarrassing for the Camerons as they had collaborated with Cromwell's representatives. However, diplomacy secured Locheil's position in the outside world, even if his by-name in the Highlands remained Am Meirleach Mór (The Great Robber).

The stay of Charles II's younger brother, James, Duke of York and Albany, in Scotland in the 1670s was important for the Camerons. The Duke impressed the conservative Highland chiefs, and particularly

STEALL GORGE
The middle part of Glen Nevis, with its combination of gorge, woodland and waterfall, has been described by the distinguished mountaineer W. H. Murray as being unique in Scotland and having more in common with a Himalayan valley than with other Highland glens.

HIGHLAND CATTLE IN GLEN NEVIS
After many years of decline, Highland cattle are making a comeback. A strong export trade to the continent aroused new interest and their value for crossing with other breeds to make hardy beef animals is better appreciated once again.

Ewen Cameron of Locheil, even if the rest of the country was not too happy with him. The two men got on well together, and this personal factor contributed to the later Jacobitism of the Camerons.

In spite of the Jacobite Risings of 1715 and 1719, the early eighteenth century was generally a period of settling down after the civil war and famine of the late seventeenth century. Donald Cameron of Locheil (the nineteenth chief), later to be known as The Gentle Locheil for sparing the citizens of Glasgow from the sacking of their town during the Forty-five, was engaged in the timber trade, based on his extensive forests along Loch Arkaig. He also had a charcoal-fired iron smelter there.

When Locheil set out on that fateful day in August 1745 to meet Prince Charles Edward, his intention was to advise him to return to France. Much against his will, however, he was won over by the Prince's charm, and possibly also by the offer of an indemnity should things go wrong. The winning over of Locheil was decisive and the rising went ahead. During the Forty-five, Locheil was an outstanding leader of his clan regiment.

Since then the history of the Camerons of Locheil has been similar to that of many chiefly families in the Highlands, except that unlike so many they still own land in Lochaber. In recent generations the family has produced distinguished public servants, not least the present chief who was made a Knight of the Thistle in 1973.

THE OWL OF STRONE

Domhnall MacFhionnlaidh nan Dan (Donald, son of Finlay, of the Songs) was born in Lochaber in about 1550 and, according to tradition, was the son of the standard bearer to Mac 'ic Iain, chief of the MacDonalds of Glencoe. His mother was from Lochaber, the daughter of a deer stalker and poet, who lived at Creag Guanach by the head of Loch Treig. On his father's death, Donald returned to Glencoe, but fell out with the chief and so went back to Lochaber, where the chief of the MacDonalds of Keppoch took him on as bard and head deer stalker, in succession to his maternal grandfather. In winter Donald was based at Fersit, a little to the North of Loch Treig, and in summer he is said to have stayed near Creag Guanach at the southern end of the loch.

GLEN NEVIS
The grass fields and woodlands of the lower part of the glen overlie relatively fertile soils, derived from an outcrop of Ballachulish limestone.

He is thought to have composed his most famous poem, or group of poems, '*Oran na Comhachaig*', in about 1585. In English the poem is known sometimes as 'The Owl of Strone' and has been described as one of the most remarkable poems in the Gaelic language.

The story of the composition of the poem is that MacDonald of Keppoch held a feast in the crannog, Tigh nam Fleadh (House of Feasts) at Eadarloch (Between Loch) in what is now, as a result of the raising of the water level, part of Loch Treig. Donald was not invited but decided to go all the same. On arriving at the chief's hall he found that the party was over. Standing alone in the dark he heard an owl hoot and felt that he and the bird shared their loneliness. He walked home to the head of Loch Treig and composed the poem. It is in the Celtic tradition of nature poetry and takes the form of a conversation with an owl, in which such subjects as the hunting of deer and the memories of past days are covered. The poem praises the chiefs of Keppoch and deals with old age, as the owl was traditionally thought to be an exceptionally long-lived bird.

Donald was also renowned for his skill with a bow and his reputation was such that the saying '*Cho cuimseach ri Domhnall MacFhionnlaidh nan Dan*' ('As accurate as Donald MacFinlay') could still be heard in Lochaber up to the 1880s. Shortly before his death, Donald's daughter saw him struggle to his feet and call for his bow on observing a particularly fine stag from the window of his house. The two of them managed to string the bow and he shot the deer. One of his last requests was that he should be buried, wrapped in the hide of the deer, in a grave by the church door at Cillechoiril, facing Cro Dhearg, a mountain south-east of Fersit. Cattle hides were of great importance in ancient religious ritual throughout the British Isles in the past. They were used for divination, sometimes based on the interpretation of dreams. Why did Donald want to be buried as if he were a seer, or was the hide part of a pre-Christian totemistic cult? Could there have been an echo of an early Celtic belief in the transmigration of souls?

MACCOLLA, MONTROSE AND THE BATTLE OF INVERLOCHY
After ravaging Argyll during the autumn and early winter of 1644, the Royalist army made its way north, pursued by the forces of the Earl of

Argyll. Eventually they reached the Great Glen and learned that an army of 5,000 men, commanded by the Earl of Seaforth, was awaiting their arrival at the northern end. Were they to be boxed in by greatly superior forces? Montrose and Alasdair MacColla decided to march on towards Cillechuimen (now Fort Augustus) and to turn south up Glen Tarff shortly before reaching it. They probably took the route now followed by the military road for part of the way before turning south to march down by the head of Glen Roy, down Glen Spean, round by Leanachan, below the lower slopes of Ben Nevis, and so to Inverlochy by the morning of 2 February 1645. They had covered forty miles (sixty-four kilometres) in a day and a night of marching through a snow-covered landscape. When one remembers that conventional armies through history have not usually managed to cover more than about fifteen miles (twenty-four kilometres) a day, one can understand the achievement of MacColla's Gaels. The Earl of Argyll's forces were deceived into thinking that their contacts with Montrose's army were only with the stragglers of a retreating force. When it came to the Royalists' attack, the Lowlanders among the Government army fled leaving the field to the Gaels. In spite of brave resistance, the Campbells were unable to withstand the fury of the Royal Army as the wedge-shaped attack formations, perfected by MacColla in the Irish wars, charged home victoriously.

Iain Lom MacDonald, the Keppoch bard, was present at the battle of Inverlochy and commemorated it in uncompromisingly savage, but brilliantly evocative verse. The remembrance of this battle, in essence yet another fratricidal struggle between Gaelic people, is usually left to Iain Lom's verse, with its description of the Campbells' eyes glazing over in death, and the savagery of the wounds they had received from the blue, sharp blades of Clan Donald; but we should remember the verse of the women, in one case a Campbell , married to a MacLean, who composed a poem in which she lamented the loss of her brothers and father on the field of Inverlochy.

There is another poem, by the widow of Campbell of Glenfeochan, which describes the terrible destruction wrought by the Royalist forces of Montrose and MacColla the previous winter, and the subsequent loss of her husband and sons.

RED DEER BESIDE LOCH ARKAIG
Late winter and a sharp westerly breeze whips up the waves at the bleak northern end of Loch Arkaig, territory of the Camerons of Lochiel. A party of stags has made its daily rendezvous with the deer stalker and is eating the food he has put out for them. The increase of deer numbers here in the west has not been so marked as in the East Highlands.

THE GREAT GLEN, GLEN AFFRIC AND STRATHGLASS

LOCH LINNHE
Loch Linnhe has been an important sea-way from earliest times: Columba sailed through on his way to negotiate with King Brude near Inverness. Currently bulk carriers use the loch to pick up aggregate from the super quarry at Glen Sanda in Ardgour.

GLEN MORE, the Great Glen, is the best example of a wrench or tear fault in the British Isles and was initiated about 300 million years ago. The Highlands north of the Great Glen slid south and west as a block. Some indication of the extent of the faulting was given when it was shown that granite from Foyers on Loch Ness-side matched that around Strontian, in the country opposite the island of Lismore at the mouth of Loch Linnhe, some sixty-five miles (105 kilometres) away.

After the fall of the Comyns, following Robert I's victory in the War of Independence (formally ended by the Treaty of Edinburgh in 1328), the Frasers, Grants and Macintoshes came to dominate the country at the north of the glen, while the MacDonalds of Glengarry and of Keppoch, and the Camerons became important in the south under the Lordship of the Isles. The rise of the Camerons continued after the end of the Lordship after 1493.

At Drumnadrochit, the A887 climbs through Glen Moriston and then descends to Loch Cluanie and so by the A87 through Kintail to Kyle of Lochalsh. Further on up the side of Loch Ness is the A831, which leads to Cannich and that beautiful group of glens: Affric, Strathfarrar and Cannich, each with magnificent remnants of Caledonian pine forest. They were identified in the 1940s as an area deserving protection as a national park, but nothing came of this far-sighted proposal. The glens' rivers flow down to Strathglass, formerly Chisholm country, to join the Beauly. Past Aigas House, now a Field Study Centre, is Eilean Aigas, situated on an island in the river. For a few years it was home to those intriguing brothers, the Sobieski-Stuarts, who did so much to create the modern myth about tartan.

GLEN AFFRIC
Glen Affric's famed beauty has survived the Affric/Farrar/Beauly Hydro-electric scheme, which was completed in 1963. To protect it, it was decided that the water level of the loch should not be raised and the need for water storage was met by the more remote Loch Mullardoch.

The Great Glen has always been an important line of communication with its string of lochs—Loch Lochy, Loch Oich and Loch Ness—linked since early in the last century by the Caledonian Canal, and never more so than in the sixth century of this millennium.

CALUM CILLE AND THE PICTS

Ever since the establishment of the Dalriadan kingdom at the beginning of the sixth century there had been sporadic warfare between the Picts and the Scots over frontiers. The Picts seem to have accepted the presence of the Dalriadans on the coast, but were determined not to let them come inland beyond the ridge of Drumalbyn.

In AD 563, Saint Columba, known to the Gaels as Calum Cille (Dove of the Church), arrived in Scotland. His mission may have been a penance for taking part in the Battle of Cul Drebene in Ulster in AD 561. Some say that he was granted Iona in 574 by his friend and ally Aidan, King of Dalriada, while others say that he and his followers were allowed to establish their monastery there by the Pictish king, Bridei Mac Maelchon.

It is likely that the purpose of Columba's visit in AD 573 to King Bridei at his capital, probably in the fort of Craig Phadrig, outside Inverness (or at what is now Urquhart Castle), was to negotiate with him on boundaries as an emissary of King Aidan, and to try to convert him and his people to Christianity.

Preparations for the journey were made. The Pictish king must have been contacted to ensure a safe conduct through his otherwise hostile territory. Columba arranged for Saint Comgall, the founder of Bangor, and Saint Canice, another Irish Pict from what is now County Down and South Antrim, to travel with him and act as interpreters.

Most of the journey to Craig Phadrig was probably done in coracles (*curaich* in Gaelic), hide-covered boats with wooden or wicker frames. Columba and his party must have left Iona and sailed east into the Sound of Lorne, then up Loch Linnhe. They would have had to disembark to follow the River Lochy into the mouth of the Great Glen itself. After this they must have carried their boats for the unnavigable parts of the journey and sailed up Loch Lochy, along Loch Oich and finally along Loch Ness.

THE CALEDONIAN CANAL

Commissioned in 1802, the canal was intended to open up the Highlands for their better economic exploitation and to make life easier for British merchant ships by allowing them to avoid the stormy waters of the northern passage and by protecting them from the threat of French warships. By the time it was completed in 1844, the canal was already obsolescent; the military threat had disappeared and steamships, generally too big for the canal and for which the difficult winds of the northern passage were not such a problem, were replacing sailing ships. In terms of its original purpose the canal was an economic disaster, but it has been a boon for fishermen, and the tourist industry.

GLEN AFFRIC

There are some 2,000 hectares (5,000 acres) of native pinewood in Glen Affric, which makes the glen an area of great ecological importance. There are also splendid areas of native pinewood in Glen Strathfarrar and Glen Cannich. Beyond Loch Affric the forest gives way to open hill and a path leads over to Kintail, only about twenty miles away to the west.

KESSOCH BRIDGE
Sunrise from the Kessoch Bridge. The new road bridge spans the Beauly Firth and replaces the ferry. Ferries were a great feature of travel in the Highlands until quite recently. Most have now been replaced by bridges.

When they arrived at the north end of Loch Ness, Columba and his companions made their way to King Bridei Mac Maelchon's fort. One can imagine Saint Columba climbing the craig to the dun of the King. Outside the fortress he celebrated vespers in spite of the efforts of Bridei's magicians, who seem to have been fearful of the effect this might have on their fellow countrymen. Columba understood this and chanted Psalm 44. 'And in the same moment his voice was, in a marvellous manner, so raised in the air like a terrible peal of thunder, that both the king and the people were filled with intolerable dread.' (Saint Adamnan's *Life of Columba*). Next, 'first imprinting the sign of the Lord's cross upon the doors, he then knocked, and laid his hand upon them. And immediately the bars were forcibly drawn back, and the doors opened of themselves with all speed. As soon as they were open, the saint entered with his associates.' Columba conversed with Bridei, but seems not to have converted him. This is emphasized by the account of the contrary wind sent by the druids to hinder Columba in his journey back down the loch, even though he was able to calm the wind, or turn it in his favour.

Columba seems to have travelled into Pictish territory several times and it is likely that he visited King Bridei more than once, particularly as the King is described as being on friendly terms with the Saint. It was at a crossing of the River Ness on one of his journeys through Pictland that Columba's encounter with a monster is recorded.

It seems that Columba and his party had crossed the river and met a funeral party on the banks of the Ness, gathered there to bury somebody whom the monster had killed. Despite the danger, Columba ordered one of his companions to swim back to the other side of the river and collect a small boat that they had left behind. Unable to resist the provocation, the monster, which had been lurking nearby on the river bed, rose to attack the swimmer. Columba made the sign of the Cross, invoked the name of God and ordered the beast away. All around were amazed by the power of the Christian God.

As Ian Finlay points out in his book *Columba*, until recent times every river and loch had some beast or other in it and it was incumbent upon any holy man worth his salt to show that he could deal with such creatures. As to the question of whether such a beast inhabits the deep waters of Loch Ness now; it used to be suggested that Nessie might be something like a plesiosaur, a survival from an earlier geological period. There are two reasons why this is improbable; first, the last Ice Age covered the whole land and scoured out any fresh water bodies. There could be no survival under these circumstances even if plesiosaurs had survived the great extinctions at the end of the Cretaceous period. Second, Loch Ness is very poor in nutrients. The volume of water capable of receiving enough sunlight to support a thriving plant life, and hence invertebrate life to maintain a lot of fish, is not enough to produce the amount of food that a large animal such as Nessie would need to survive.

THE KEPPOCH MURDER

The Keppoch murder is a curious incident in that it stands fairy-tale logic on its head. It has the intriguing ingredients of a young chief, a murderous cousin who turns out to be preferred by the clan, and two poets, one of them the sister of the victims.

The story runs thus; the young sons of Domhnall Glas XI (Grey Donald), Chief of the MacDonells of Keppoch, were sent to be educated in France and returned in 1663. While they were away their cousin, Alasdair Buidhe, Tutor of Keppoch, managed the land occupied by the clan. The return of the young chief and his brother became unwelcome to the clan when it was suspected that the young chief was contemplating a deal with their would-be landlord, Macintosh, that would threaten the way the clansmen held their land. Worse still, the young chief, also called Alasdair, feuded with MacDonald of Inverlair and Alasdair Buidhe. A squabble at a banquet became the scene of the murder of the young chief and his brother.

The clan showed what it thought of the killings by taking as chief Alasdair Buidhe, whose sons were alleged to have been involved in the murder, but had escaped. There was little inclination to avenge the murder of the two brothers, either from among the MacDonells of Keppoch or elsewhere. However, Iain Lom, the Bard of Keppoch, was indignant about the failure to avenge the killings and visited a number of MacDonald chiefs urging them to take action against the murderers. In the end, MacDonald of Sleat provided Iain Lom with some men. The

URQUHART CASTLE
The remains, as we see them today, date from about 1200. It was held from 1228 by Alan Durward, but by 1304 was in the hands of the Comyns, for whom the Chisolms may have been keepers. King Robert I's forces destroyed the castle in 1307. During the reign of James IV the castle was repaired and the King gave it and the lordship of Urquhart to John Grant of Freuchie. By 1715 it was once more in ruins.

murderers' house at Inverlair (in Glen Spean) was surrounded and the seven brothers were killed and decapitated. Their heads were put into a bag and they were taken by Iain Lom to be shown to MacDonald of Glengarry. On the way to Glengarry castle, the heads are said to have grumbled from within the bag in which they were being carried and Iain Lom said to them '*Ubh, ubh! Nach còrd sibh 's gur cloinn chàirdean sibh fhein.*' ('Oh dear! Can you not get on, and you related to each other?') When they reached the well on the side of Loch Oich he took the heads out of the bag and washed them before presenting them to Glengarry. To this day the well where the heads were washed is known as the Tobar nan Ceann (The Well of the Heads). In about 1815, Alasdair Ranaldson, Chief of Glengarry, whose portrait by Sir Henry Raeburn hangs in the Scottish National Gallery in Edinburgh, had a monument erected to commemorate this incident.

Talking heads and magic wells bring with them a recollection of Iron Age head-hunting habits. Suddenly, we are among the same people that Caesar and other Roman writers described in Gaul more than 1,500 years before. The inscriptions on the monument at Loch Oich commemorate a chief's view of the incident. It is significant that Alasdair Ranaldson was responsible for wasting his estate and bringing eviction and misery to his clansmen tenants at a time when the power of landowners was pre-eminent.

THE LAMENT FOR WILLIAM CHISHOLM

The Chisholms were of Anglo-Norman origin and held land in Strathglass, Glen Affric and Glen Cannich. The 'Lament for William Chisholm' emphasizes the terrible consequences of the Rising of 1745 for the family of one who took part in the affair. The Chisholms of Strathglass were led into the rising on the Jacobite side under the command of the chief's youngest son, Roderick. William Chisholm was standard bearer of his clan at the Battle of Culloden and was killed there. His death was lamented by his widow, Christina Ferguson from Contin in Ross-shire. Here are three verses from this great and tragic song, as it was recorded from the late Roderick MacKinnon by Dr Campbell of Canna. I am grateful to Dr Campbell for permission to publish this part of the poem.

THE WELL OF THE HEADS
This monument to the victims of the Keppoch murder was erected in 1812 by Alasdair Ranaldson, Chief of the MacDonells of Glengarry. Alasdair was a descendant of the Glengarry who, by providing the poet Iain Lom MacDonald with assistants, ensured that the murder of the young chief of Keppoch and his brother would be avenged.

Och, a Thearlaich òig Stiùbhart'
Se do chùis rinn mo léireadh,
Thug thu bhuam gach nì bh'agam
Anns a' chogadh 'nad adhbhar;
Cha bu chrodh, 's cha bu chaoraich,
Tha mi caoi, ach mo cheudghaol,
'Sann a dh'fhàg thu mi'm aonar,
Gun sian dha'n saoghal ach léine,

Mo rùn geal òg

Bha mi treis ann am barail
Gum bu mhaireann mo cheudghaol,
'S gun digeadh tu fhathast
Le aighear,'s le faoilteachd;
G'eil an t-àm air dol seachad
'S chan fhaic mi fear t'aogais,
'S gus an téid mi fo'n talamh
A chaoidh cha dhealaich do ghaol
  rium

Mo rùn geal òg

Co nis a thogas an claidheamh
No nì a'chathair a'lìonadh?
'S gann gur h-e a th'air m'aire,
O nach maireann mo cheudghaol;
De mar gheibh mi o m'nàdur
A bhith 'g àicheadh na's miann leum
Is mo thochradh cho làidir
Bhith cur an àite mo rìgh mhath?

Mo rùn geal òg.

O, young Charles Stewart,
your cause has brought grief to me;
The war fought in your cause
has taken all I possessed;
It is not (plundered) cattle, or sheep,
that I lament, but my first love,
You have left me alone with nothing
in the world but a shirt,

My fair young love.

For a time I believed that
my first love was alive,
and that you would return yet
with joy and rejoicing;
but the time has gone past
and I do not see anyone of your
  likeness;
Until I am buried
love of you will never leave me

My fair young love.

Who now will raise the sword
Or fill the throne?
That is scarcely on my mind,
since my first love no longer lives;
How shall I, from my own nature,
deny my wish, when my desire to put
my fair young love in the place
of my good king is so strong?

My fair young love.

TARTAN—THE CLAN CHIC

In the National Gallery of Scotland in Edinburgh there is a painting of 'Venus and Mars' by the Venetian artist Paolo Veronese. Draped over Venus's lap is a piece of tartan cloth. It is a black and yellow check with an overstripe and looks, from a distance, like the tartan known nowadays as MacLeod of Harris. The truth is that tartan is not an exclusively Scottish, let alone, Highland phenomenon. Wherever humans have learned to weave they have produced checks. The difference in Scotland, and particularly in the Highlands, is that tartan became important as a symbol. When the Jacobites of Edinburgh adopted tartan as a token of their support for Prince Charles Edward Stuart in 1745 they demonstrated something that the Government was to recognize in 1746. The Disarming Act of that year banned the wearing of the kilt and the use of tartan, except in the military service of the Crown.

Many examples, from portraits in the Scottish National Portrait Gallery in Edinburgh, or in private collections, or in the reports of visitors to the Highlands, show that there was no idea of personal or family right to particular tartans. However, it was the case that tartan often indicated where someone came from because inhabitants of a district tended to weave similar patterns. As we have seen, clan territories were by no means always occupied exclusively by one clan.

The wearing of the kilt by the new Highland regiments in the period after the Forty-five encouraged young men to join the British army, in

GLEN GARRY
Much afforestation was carried out by the newly established Forestry Commission in the 1920s and 1930s. Scots Pine, Douglas Fir and the spruces were favoured at first, but more recently Sitka Spruce has predominated. There is also some native pinewood in the glen.

part to avoid the humiliation of not being allowed to wear their native dress. However, in spite of persecution, the kilt continued to be worn in the Highlands, although less and less. The knowledge of weaving the traditional tartans seems to have died out in the generation which followed the Disarming Act.

In 1822, Sir Walter Scott stage-managed the successful visit of George IV to Edinburgh. Chiefly landowners were asked to turn out their followers, all dressed in the ancient garb. What was to be done? There was recourse to the famous firm of Wilson of Bannockburn which had a pattern book showing the tartans that it wove. Many of these were called such names as 'White Wellington', 'Robin Hood', or 'Caledonia'. A clan chief could choose a tartan, and, who knows, it might become his for ever. Many of these tartans are now known by the names of famous clans and worn all over the world as such. The royal visit stimulated new interest in tartans and Highland dress and prepared the ground for the phenomenon of the Sobieski-Stuarts.

This mysterious pair first appeared in Scotland in the 1820s. They claimed to be the grandsons of Prince Charles Edward, and it was agreed that they had a very strong Stuart look about them. At all events the brothers persuaded a great many people at the time that they were of royal descent through the exiled Stuarts. They went to live at Eilean Aigas in Strathglass in 1838 under the patronage of the Lord Lovat of the day. There they learned Gaelic and researched the customs, dress and history, including the environmental history, of the old Highlands. Much of their scholarship has been corroborated, but controversy surrounded the publication of their beautifully produced book *Vestiarium Scoticum* in 1842, in which a large number of tartans were reproduced. The brothers claimed that the authority for the antiquity of many of the tartans in their book came from a document dating from the sixteenth century. However, they were never able to produce this document, and it seems likely that, for the most part, they either invented the tartans themselves or consulted the pattern books of Messrs Wilson of Bannockburn. Many clan chiefs, knowing no better, accepted *Vestiarium Scoticum* as authoritative and so many of the tartans described today as belonging to specific clans or families have no more authentication than the largely spurious attributions of the Sobieski-Stuarts.

LOCH GARRY
The outline of Loch Garry resembles that of Scotland, but this has only been the case since the shoreline was changed by a hydro-electric scheme. Salmon now reach the loch by a Borland fish pass in the Invergarry Dam. This enables them to get from Loch Oich in the Great Glen to their spawning grounds in the River Garry and the other rivers of the Loch Garry catchment area.

MORVERN TO MOIDART AND ARISAIG

THE NAME MORVERN comes from the Gaelic *Morbhairne*, meaning the great gap. It is the country west of Loch Sunart and Glen Tarbert. Much of Morvern is overlain by basalt, which culminates in fine cliffs at Ardtornish on the Sound of Mull. Tarbert means an isthmus in the sense of a portage. The name is found at Tarbet on Loch Lomond side, and at Tarbert at the head of Loch Fyne. Moidart is renowned as the country of the MacDonalds of Clanranald, while the country round Loch Sunart (with its quota of fish farms) was famous for its oak woods, *Suaineart ghorm an daraich* (Green Sunart of the oak trees). Sunart is a name of Norse derivation and means Sween's Fjord. Local tradition says that Somerled the Great defeated a Viking called Torquil at the place that bears his name—Acharacle (*Ath Tharracuil* means Torquil's ford). Morvern is the land where, traditionally, Somerled had his first successes against the Norse.

To the west lies Ardnamurchan, home for some years to Alasdair MacMhaighstir Alasdair, when he was biding his time against the day when his Prince would summon him and put the world to rights.

On 4 August 1745, Prince Charles Edward Stuart landed at Loch nan Uamh in Arisaig to begin the rising that ended in disaster the following 16 April on the field of Culloden.

OAKWOODS OF THE HIGHLANDS

At the time of their greatest extent, about 8,000 years ago, the Highland pine forests stretched from the north coast of Scotland down through the Central Valley and into the Southern Uplands. The wetter climate that followed brought conditions to the West Highlands that favoured the colonization of what had been pine ground by deciduous trees. Oak forest developed and with it an assembly of subsidiary trees and plants. Within the forest mosaic there were birches, holly and hazel

LOCH MOIDART
A ruined jetty on the loch is a reminder that this area was once the centre of the sea-girt possessions of the MacDonalds of Clanranald which stretched over the Minch to include Uist.

(hazel sometimes as part of the shrub understorey and sometimes as a canopy forming species in its own right). Elsewhere there were wych elms, ash, rowan, aspen, alder and, occasionally, yew. Birch woods and willow prevailed in the Northern Highlands.

Remnants of the oak forest are widespread throughout the Central and West Highlands. They survive along the southern shores of Loch Earn and Loch Tay. They are present along the shores of Loch Etive at Bonawe, and in Appin. Further north they are to be found by Loch Sunart and in Moidart, on the north-east shores of Loch Maree and into Sutherland.

There used to be great forests along the sides of Loch Arkaig and Loch Ness. The accounts of the Masters of Works for building and repairing royal palaces and castles report the transport of oak, by ship from Lochaber, for use at the Palace of Holyrood in Edinburgh in the years 1535-6.

In the North-West Highlands, management of the oak woods for coppice from which to make charcoal had begun in 1607 when Sir George Hay, a Lowland entrepreneur, started his iron bloomeries beside Loch Maree. In spite of the felling, and the extension of grazing into the areas that had been cut, the oak woods were able to regenerate. It may be that light stocking rates of cattle and sheep enabled regeneration to go on in a way that became impossible in later times with heavier stocking.

Throughout the estates of the dukes of Argyll, from at least the eighteenth century, leases were made to ensure that the oak woods were exploited and managed in such a way as to ensure their survival. The woods at Glen Nant near Bonawe, where an iron smelter was set up in the 1750s, are a case in point. Livestock were kept out and we owe the existence of these woods to this form of industrial management. The area of oak woodland south of Loch Etive actually expanded as a result of charcoal burning for iron smelting.

Oak bark for the leather tanning industry was another important product of coppiced woodland. From the middle of the eighteenth century the oak woods on the shores of Loch Lomond were being managed on twenty- to thirty-year coppice rotations, as were many other oak woods through Perthshire, Dunbartonshire and Argyll, to supply this industry.

THE ROAD TO ARISAIG
Birch scrub flourishes near the line of the old drove road that led from Arisaig by Glen Finnan, past Loch Eil, Spean Bridge, to the head of Loch Treig and so eventually by Rannoch and Glen Ogil to Crieff.

GLEN FINNAN VIADUCT
An early concrete structure, the viaduct was built by Robert MacAlpine at the beginning of the twentieth century to carry the West Highland Railway, of which Mallaig is the railhead. The line starts from Glasgow and runs by Rannoch and Fort William to Mallaig. The town owes its existence to the fishing industry, at present (1994) going through one of its periodic depressions. This time the depression is due to overfishing.

LOCH MORAR
At 310 metres (1,020 feet) Loch Morar is the deepest body of fresh water in the British Isles. It has a number of islands, one of which was used as a place of refuge by Lord Lovat during the Forty-five when he could not make up his mind which side to support. He was captured there on 2 June 1946 by a landing party led by the notorious Captain Fergusson and paid for his dissimulation with his head.

Further north, from the sixteenth century, the MacDonalds of Clanranald were managing their oak woods in Moidart to provide timber for the *birlinns*, the galleys which ensured their power at sea in the west. By the eighteenth century they were managing their woods in similar fashion to the Campbells in Argyll.

Most coppicing in the Highlands had come to an end by about a century ago. As the eighteenth century went by, coke was used increasingly in England for the smelting of iron, and the justification for its transport from, for example, Cumbria to the West Highlands gradually diminished. The production of tannin from the oak woods of Argyll and Perthshire ceased as other processes made the older systems obsolete.

The management of the oak woods for coppice to produce charcoal or tanbark ensured the survival of many woods, even if as impoverished relics, but some were lost. The woods were always at the mercy of the market and of their owners. When the value of coppice was high (as it was during the Napoleonic Wars) the oak itself was safe after a fashion, and less important species would be cut out to favour its growth. However, if the value of the ground as grazing for sheep was greater than its value as woodland, it might be let for grazing with serious consequences for the wood's ability to regenerate. The general failure in the West Highlands to keep some standard trees (that is to say trees that were allowed to grow straight and tall rather than being coppiced) meant that where woods have survived it is usually as scrub. If the practice of encouraging standards or maiden trees had been followed, those woods in which growth is not limited by exposure or height above sea-level would not look or be scrubby at all. They would look more like the magnificent managed oak forests of Germany.

CLAN DONALD AND THE LORDSHIP OF THE ISLES

Somerled the Great, Somhairle Mac Gille Bhride 'ic Gille Adhomhnain, King of the Isles, died in battle near Renfrew in 1164 fighting Malcolm IV's forces. Somerled's Gaelic ancestry can be traced back to the ninth-century chief Godfrey MacFergus, who came from Ireland to help Kenneth MacAlpin establish himself in AD 843 as King of Alba, the united kingdom of Picts and Scots. Somerled's ancestry is traced in less detail beyond Godfrey MacFergus to Colla Uais, descended from the semi-mythical Conn of the Hundred Battles. Somerled's grandson, Donald, son of his second son, Reginald, was the progenitor of the MacDonalds.

From the time of Somerled the Lordship of the Isles seems to have rotated among the senior branches of his descendants, until the fourteenth century when it became settled on one line, Clan Donald. One of the first references to a Lord of the Isles is in a charter of 1354, where John MacDonald of Islay is described as *Dominus de Insularum*. From that time the Lordship ran formally until its destruction by the Crown towards the end of the fifteenth century. In practice, it continued until 1545 and the death of Donald Dubh, great-great-grandson of Donald, second Lord of the Isles.

The MacDonald Lordship of the Isles gave that clan a special position in Gaelic culture. The flourishing of stone carving drew its inspiration from their rule, as did the blossoming of poetry, represented in the collection known as the *Book of the Dean of Lismore*.

The chiefs of the different branches are praised in numerous songs through to the eighteenth century. The Johns of Moidart, Domhnall Gorm of Sleat, Alasdair of Glengarry: they are mentioned time and again in the songs of the Gaels. Alasdair MacColla Chiotaich, his father Colla Ciotach Mac Ghilleasbuig, Colla nam Bo (Coll of the Cows), Chief of Keppoch in 1689 (who was said to have gambled with the devil while in Rome and come away unscathed).

In the end the Lordship was unable to continue to provide the political stability that the area under its hegemony needed, and its destruction left the West Highlands open to the terrible period of *Linn nan Creach* (The Age of the Forays). Shaken by the Crown, which supported the expansionist Campbells, the Lordship fell prey to that clan's ambitions. Based in the Southern Highlands, the Campbells had seen clearly where the future lay and how to use the political system to their advantage while the divided branches of Clan Donald had remained locked in their western fastnesses.

It was said that the MacDonald gentry of Moidart in the eighteenth century knew more of what was going on in Rome and Madrid than they did of the events in Edinburgh and London. Unfortunately for them, it was a period when they needed to know what was happening in the power centres of the British Isles.

KEILLS CROSS
The church at Keills, which lies a little to the north of the village at Loch Aline, was founded by Columba. This fine cross stands outside, overlooking the Sound of Mull. On the other side of Loch Aline is Ardtornish Castle, another fortress of the Lords of the Isles.

CASTLE TIORAM
Contemporary with Mingary in Ardnamurchan, Castle Tioram is a castle of enclosure of the fourteenth century and was part of the MacRuaris' possessions until the murder of Ranald MacRuari. It then passed to his sister Amy, wife of John, Lord of the Isles, until her divorce from him in 1350. Later it became the headquarters of the MacDonalds of Clanranald until it was burnt during the 1715 Rising.

The pre-eminence of the kingdom of the Isles and of Clan Donald, taken together, lasted from 1100 to 1550 by one measure, and even the most strictly defined period of the Lordship gives them a couple of hundred years (1300–1500)—not bad by modern standards.

JACOBITISM AND THE FORTY-FIVE

Although the earlier Stewart monarchs had sometimes behaved in a destructive way towards their Highland people, the personal loyalty which James VII and II had inspired allowed Prince Charles Edward's cause to become a vehicle for those who saw Stewart legitimacy as a bastion in the defence of the old Gaelic culture, and of religious toleration. This was already threatened by the religious, social and economic changes of the time. Part of the threat was the adherence of the great Clan Campbell to the Protestant cause and so its commitment to the new order.

By 1745 enthusiasm for a rising had diminished but, in spite of the lack of military backing from France, Prince Charles Edward, grandson of James VII and II, was able to persuade enough unwilling chiefs to join him in starting the rising.

The recruitment of the fighting men of the Jacobite clans to the cause was not easy either. Many had to be recruited forcibly but, as many of the soldiers of the Government army had themselves been pressed into service, there was nothing uniquely wicked in compelling men to serve in the Jacobite army. What did these men think of the cause for which they were to fight? To some extent the opinions of the chiefs about Stewart legitimacy must have prevailed, and it seems likely that most Jacobite Highlanders feared that the economic and political changes then spreading through the country would destroy their society. The widespread millenarian belief in the prophesy of Thomas the Rhymer (the thirteenth-century seer, who, according to myth, is buried in Tomnahurich near Inverness) that there would be a successful national uprising, followed by a Gaelic revival, may have given impetus to the Gaels who joined the Prince's cause.

There were other reasons in Scotland for the existence of Jacobitism. The Treaty of Union of 1707 had been extremely unpopular at the time of its enactment. Even among those who had supported it there were

THE SEVEN MEN OF MOIDART
The predecessors of these beech trees on the north shore of Loch Moidart were planted to commemorate the seven men who accompanied Prince Charles Edward when he landed in Scotland in August 1745.

A BUZZARD
The number of buzzards in Scotland has been increasing in the last few years, possibly because recent mild winters have enabled more rabbits and small rodents to survive, thereby providing the buzzards with a supply of food.

many who had thought that it was necessary only because there had seemed to be no choice. English power had excluded the Scots from the new trade routes to North America and the East, and had contributed to the disaster of the Darien Scheme (a failed attempt to establish a trading colony in the isthmus of Panama), which had brought so much misery to the country.

Union with England was meant to end the exclusion of Scottish merchants from English markets overseas. However, in the period following the Union of the Parliaments, the effect of becoming part of a Customs' Union dominated by the English meant that many old markets throughout Europe, with which Scots merchants had traded for centuries, were closing to them. Towns like Inverness had been better off in 1701 than they were in the middle years of the century.

Much support for the Jacobite cause came form the many Episcopalians in Scotland, as it did from the rather fewer Roman Catholics. Both of these groups suffered from discrimination which had the effect of strengthening their Jacobite leanings. In addition, there was simple regret at the loss of an independence that had been so bitterly fought for over the centuries.

ALASDAIR MACMHAIGHSTIR ALASDAIR

Alasdair MacMhaighstir Alasdair, or Alexander MacDonald, was born in about 1698, probably at Dalilea on the north shore of Loch Sheil. He was related to the chiefly family of MacDonald of Clanranald, whose stronghold was Castle Tioram in Moidart. In about 1727 he married Jane, the daughter of MacDonald of Dalness in Glen Etive, whom he may have met on his journeys to and from Glasgow University where he was a student.

Alexander MacDonald was a great Gaelic poet. His best known works include the magnificent sea song '*Birlinn Chlann Raghnail*' ('Clanranald's Galley'), the account of a voyage from Uist to Carrickfergus in Northern Ireland, and the lyrical '*A'dol thar Allt an t-siùcair*' ('Crossing the Sugar Burn'). He is remembered, too, for his enthusiastic involvement in the Jacobite cause and held the rank of captain in the Clanranald regiment in the Forty-five. He fought throughout that campaign and left a description which

LOCH EILT
The long, narrow loch is a throughway with a road on its north side and a railway to the south. The road has an ancient history: once an old coffin road (with resting cairns), it was later a drove road during the centuries when cattle trade flourished. Today the A830(T) is used for the transport of fish from Mallaig to the markets in the south and gives access to the crofts and caravan sites of Morar.

GLEN FINNAN MONUMENT
This monument at the head of Loch Sheil was erected by Alexander MacDonald of Glenaladale in 1814, in memory of the Highlanders who rose to the Jacobite cause in 1745. The island in the loch is mentioned in Alasdair MacMhaigstir's Alasdair's poem 'Birlinn Chlann Raghnaill' ('Clanranald's Galley') as the source of wood for the galley's oars. On the north side of the loch is Gaskin Wood, from which the MacDonalds of Clanranald cut timber to build their galleys.

included an account of the arrival of Prince Charles Edward in Moidart, at which MacDonald met the Prince and became the Prince's Gaelic teacher.

MacDonald played an important, though indefinable, part in the events which led to Prince Charles Edward's arrival. In the years that preceded the rising, verse by Alasdair was sent to Aeneas MacDonald, banker in Paris to the Jacobite Court, to be passed on to the Prince. These poems were incitements to the clans to join in a rising to restore the House of Stewart. At least one of these poems listed the clans that would rise for the Prince, and included the Campbells.

It seems likely that these propagandist poems played a part in encouraging the Prince's belief that all the Highland clans, even the Campbells, would rise and fight for him. In this, and later on the field of Culloden, he was a victim of his own wishful thinking and upbringing.

LOCH SUNART

Loch Sunart is a sea loch and, with Glen Tarbert, cuts Morvern off from the rest of the mainland. The exchange of water by the ebb and flow of the tide is not as great as in other sea lochs. This has given rise to pollution problems because the accumulation of waste from the fish farms in the loch cannot be swept away by the tides so effectively.

FISH FARMING

In the last twenty years fish farming has developed from a small-scale undertaking into a massive industry, turning over millions of pounds sterling annually and providing much needed employment in areas of the West Highlands. A recent survey has shown that about one third of the men living in the parish of Morvern is employed in fish farming.

The first fish farms in this wave of colonization started to appear in the late 1970s, and as the experimental nature of these enterprises wore off many more were set up. Most of these farmed salmon. More recently mussels, scallops and oysters are being farmed. The whole thing seemed splendidly straightforward. There was no need to gain planning permission from the local government's planning department; and the Crown Estate Commissioners, who are responsible for controlling the coastal bottom, were delightfully accommodating about granting permission for the establishment of fish farms. For a while this bonanza lasted. However, the sight of so many lochs with their clusters of fish farms upset visitors, and there was more to it than the objections of those with merely aesthetic sensitivities. Yachtsmen found that sheltered anchorages were no longer available in time of storm and the news that fish farmers were treating their salmon with highly toxic substances to kill the sea lice that infest them in salt water upset conservationists and those involved in shell fisheries.

These concerns have since been heightened by others. Up to ten per cent of the fishmeal fed to salmon in their cages falls through as waste to the bottom of the lochs, as do all the faeces. Where there is insufficient exchange of sea water due to lack of tidal flow, as in Loch Sunart, this allows the waste food to build up and causes pollution, threatening the natural flora and fauna of the sea bed. Escapes of domestic salmon have also worried people as they fear farmed salmon might infect wild salmon with diseases. (In actuality it seems to be the other way about; fish in pens catch diseases and parasites from wild fish.) There is the likelihood, too, that the genetic integrity of stocks of wild salmon will be harmed as a result of interbreeding with domestic salmon. Certain attributes considered desirable in domestic stock (like docility) might turn out to be undesirable in the wild. Norwegian experience has shown this to be the case.

Then there are the predators. For the seals of the west, the presence of huge numbers of salmon so close at hand is a sore temptation to try to break into the cages, as it is for otters. Ospreys and herons are astonished at the abundance of food. Humans do not like rivals and so it is out with the gun. Cormorants, shags and divers (loons) get stuck in the mesh of salmon pens, especially when these contain early post-smolts (adolescent salmon).

Naturally fish farming is not without its advantages, particularly in providing employment. Critics, however, say that while this may be true for the smaller-scale enterprises, it does not necessarily hold for larger ones. Worse, if there is a downturn in the market for farmed salmon, the bigger firms, it is said, are more likely to sell up, or to shut down their operations and sack their labour forces.

Inevitably there are fierce controversies, often within communities, between traditional fishermen, who see the farmed fish as a threat, and those who benefit from the work. Between them are the environmental complications—predators and prey, the insecticide 'Nuvan', pollution of the sea floor, visual pollution, escapes and genetic pollution of the valuable indigenous wild stock. If these problems can be resolved fish farming should have an important future in the West Highlands.

A BUILDING NEAR INVERAILORT
Stone is the standard building material in a country where timber has come to be in relatively short supply. Through the centuries masons have had to make do with whatever the local stone offered in the way of possibilities. Accordingly, the domestic architecture of each part of the Highlands reflects its underlying or surrounding geology, as does this ruined building, built mainly of local Moine Schist.

$\mathcal{K}$INTAIL TO LOCH BROOM

THE COULIN PINEWOODS

The pines of Wester Ross are genetically distinct from the other native pines in the Highlands. An explanation for this seems to be that the pines of the Central and Eastern Highlands returned by the North Sea land bridge in early post-Glacial times, but that those found in Wester Ross survived in refugia off what is now the coast of Ireland. They then returned after the retreat of the ice, having spread during the previous inter-glacial from a more southerly European source. Auvergne has been suggested as a possible provenance.

FROM KILDONNAN ON THE SHORES of Little Loch Broom in the north, to Glen Elchaig in Kintail in the south, this land has strong associations with the Christian missionaries of the generations after Saint Columba. They established many churches and the lands of the monastery of Saint Maol Rubha at Applecross (founded in AD 673), for example, stretched from Loch Duich to Loch Broom. Much later, in about 1230, a descendant of the hereditary lay abbots of Applecross, Fearchar Mac an t-Sagairt (Mactaggart means son of the priest) was granted the Earldom of Ross for services to the Crown.

The Earldom of Ross, of which this country formed part, succumbed to the Lords of the Isles only briefly between the time when Alexander, Lord of the Isles, gained it in 1436 and his son, John, renounced it in 1476, but the effort expended in gaining the Earldom may have cost the Lordship complete control of its southern marches in Argyll and so made the way easier for the Campbells.

By about 1600 Wester Ross was dominated by the MacKenzies of Kintail, but for some 300 years before that a number of smaller clans had held different parts of the area. The MacNicols (or Nicolsons) held the country around Loch Broom. The Clann Anndreis (Gillanders) were around Gairloch. The Mathesons held Loch Alsh, and the MacKenzies held only Kintail. The MacRaes were constables of the Castle of Eilean Donan for the MacKenzies, and their name is one of the best known of the clans from Kintail.

North, beyond Loch Kishorn, is the peninsula of Applecross, to which access could only formerly be obtained by the steep Bealach nam Bo (Pass of the Cows). Now the old road (reputedly once the worst road in Scotland) is much improved, although still steep enough to impress, and there is a new road that follows the peninsula north by Shieldaig. Further north is Torridon with its ancient sandstone and those wonderful mountains, Liathach (The Grey One), Ben Eighe, topped with a cap of quartzite, Slioch looking over Loch Maree, and an Teallach (the anvil), above Little Loch Broom, where that visionary conservationist, Frank Fraser Darling, studied his herd of red deer.

Ullapool, on the shores of Loch Broom, has long been established as a fishing station and Loch Broom itself became known as the starting point for many emigrant ships (of which perhaps the terrible voyage of the *Hector* in 1773 is best known) bound for Canada and the United States of America.

THE CALEDONIAN FOREST

After the last ice age, the plants gradually came back and the pine forests of mainland Europe crowded across the land bridge joining it to Britain and forged their way through to Scotland. It has turned out, however, that the sub-species of pine in Scotland is genetically distinct from the sub-species that came across the land bridge into England, and that the northern limit of the pine in England was probably about 150 miles (240 kilometres) south of the southernmost limit of the post-glacial extent of the pine in Scotland.

From where, then, did the Scots Pine come? The answer may never be known for certain, but recent research suggests that the native Scots Pine of the north-west survived the full rigour of the last glaciation in refugia. There may have been a number of these ice-free areas in peninsulas off the west of Ireland. Then, as the ice retreated and the climate warmed, the soil improved enough for the growth of pines. Released from their isolated sanctuaries, and facing no competition from rival species, the Scots Pine was given full opportunity for expression.

At their greatest expansion, about 8,000 years ago, the pine forests of the Highlands probably ranged from Loch Shin in Sutherland to Loch Lomond in the south, and from Knoydart in the west across to Buchan in the east. However, around 1,000 years later, the climate went into a wetter and colder phase and blanket peat started to form, making conditions for the regeneration of the pine woods in the areas of higher rainfall of the West and Northern Highlands increasingly difficult. Eventually, regeneration became possible only on slopes which were too steep for peat to form on.

RONA AND THE NORTH END OF RAASAY
Raasay, photographed here from Applecross, was home of a branch of the MacLeods. Two of Sorley Maclean's best-known poems are about the island—the 'Coilltean Ratharsair' (Woods of Raasay) and 'Hallaig', where past generations rise and fuse with the birchwoods of the island; the people and their environment as one.

APPLECROSS
This row of fishermen's cottages in Applecross, Wester Ross, was built in the nineteenth century. The Gaelic name for Applecross is 'A 'Chromraich', meaning 'The Sanctuary', appropriate both for Applecross's history as a religious settlement and for its relatively good soils in comparison with those of the surrounding countryside. Fishing and tourism are the main activities today.

THE TORRIDON HILLS *(overleaf)*
Ben Alligin (the Jewel Mountain) appears on the left through cloud, which conceals Liathach (the Grey One) on the right. The hills of Torridon are formed from the 600 million year old Torridonian sandstone which, in the case of Liathach and some others, is capped with Cambrian quartzite.

THE KIRKTON OF LOCH DUICH
The Church and neighbouring loch were named after St Duthac (fl. 1050). There is a story of an old man who accompanied a funeral procession to the church. Tired by the long walk, he sat down by the side of the road and composed a song, 'Theid mi dhachaidh Chro Chinn t-Saile' ('I will return home to the Cro of Kintail'). The melody is a well-known pipe tune.

It also seems likely that humans were already affecting the capacity of the woods to regenerate, and even influencing the character of the forests themselves by the use of fire to make clearings, where the growth of heather and grasses would encourage game.

In the Central and Eastern Highlands the forests remained largely unaffected by the changed climate. The rainfall remained low enough for the trees to continue to regenerate. Even at Loch Maree much pine forest remained and with it enough oak to tempt Sir George Hay to start on his exploitation of the region's forests for the manufacture of iron in 1607.

THE BLIND HARPER AND THE ROLE OF THE CHIEFS

The earliest musical instrument of the Gaels of Scotland and Ireland was a form of harp. By the twelfth century this had evolved in Scotland into a triangular harp, or *clarsach*, the Celtic harp with which we are familiar. The harpers were senior figures in the clan society of the medieval Highlands.

One of the last great harpers to MacLeod of Dunvegan was Ruaidhri MacMhuirich, known as an Clarsair Dall (the Blind Harper). He was born on the Isle of Lewis in about 1656, and was sent to Ireland, as was the custom, for his musical education. On his return, he was appointed minstrel by Iain Breac MacLeod of Dunvegan, and was given the farm of Tota Mor in Glenelg in payment for his services as harper.

He is known above all for the '*Oran do MhacLeòid Dhùn Bhegain*' ('Song to MacLeod of Dunvegan'). Apart from the beauty of the song, it is an important social document. It laments the frequent absence of the chief in Edinburgh and the extravagance of the demands that his new way of life places on the clan. The equivalent of seven rent collections are borrowed to pay for a horse and saddle. The poet has more to say. The chief is gambling away his inheritance and falling into debt. Harpers and bards were often spokesmen for the clan, expressing feelings others did not like, or dare, to voice. They travelled about the country and heard what was going on throughout the Highlands. Where the question of debt arose, they would remember notorious cases such as that of the MacLeans of Duart. In this case the MacLeans' debts had been taken over by the Campbells who foreclosed on the

EILEAN DONAN CASTLE
As with all good defensive sites, Eilean Donan has a long history of occupation. A prehistoric fort preceded the medieval tower built in the fourteenth century. The castle passed into the hands of the MacKenzies early in the sixteenth century and the MacRaes occupied it on their behalf as constables. In 1739 Eilean Donan was occupied for a short time by a Spanish garrison who were forced to surrender after being bombarded by the Royal Navy. From then it remained a ruin until early this century when it was restored by Colonel MacRae-Gilstrap.

MacLeans and invaded their territory militarily. As a result, after prolonged warfare, the MacLeans lost Morvern, Mull and Tiree.

The times were changing and the chiefs faced a dilemma. From the middle of the seventeenth century the great chiefs, such as the Earls of Argyll, the MacDonalds of Sleat, the Camerons of Locheil and the MacLeods of Dunvegan, saw themselves as players on the national stage. To do this it was necessary to go to Court. The Campbells, as we have seen, had come to a position of enormous power by a careful working of the political system. It was madness for important chiefs to ignore the Court and so they had to spend more time away from their lands and people. In England the Gaelic aristocrats came across a nobility that was rich beyond the dreams of the Gaels, yet pride demanded that they should not be outdone by the English and Lowland lords. The Union of the Parliaments in 1707 made the position still worse because the power of patronage of Crown and Parliament had now both abandoned Scotland.

On the other hand, the people wanted their chief to rule over them at home; to act as arbiter in disputes, to lead them, and to entertain in the traditional way. Hence the complaints about the chief's extravagance abroad, expressed by the harper as voice of the clan when MacLeod came home. The welcoming hall, the silver cups and candlesticks, wine, brandy, great feasting, the playing of backgammon and dice, the sound of song and harp were all expected of the chief at home. The produce of the land was then seen to be kept within the local economy, rather than being exported to support an extravagant way of life that seemed only to benefit the tradesmen of London, and to result in debt.

EMIGRATION

Visits to the Lowlands and, above all, to England suggested to the Highland aristocracy that farming could be practised differently and far more profitably than it was at home. So, in 1730, the Duke of Argyll decided to reorganize his farms in Argyll and Mull, and arranged for them to be re-let on a more commercial footing. Without the middle men that the tacksmen had been, tenant farmers would surely be able to pay higher rents. Not only that but the new tenants would be asked to pay cash instead of paying their rent in kind. Out went the old

FEARNMORE

Fearnmore is at the north-west corner of the Applecross peninsula. Like many crofting settlements there are several generations of dwelling on the same site: a modern, slated house; the cast-off 'black house', now with a corrugated iron roof, but formerly thatched; and an even older building, now in ruins.

WATERFALL BESIDE LITTLE LOCH BROOM

The water tumbles into Little Loch
Broom opposite Kildonan where,
buried in a mound, lies the Viking
Princess, Dubh a'Ghiubhais. Legend
has it that, to please her father, she
came to Scotland in the guise of
a great white bird and set fire to
the pine forest by touching trees
with her wing.

tacksmen, the gentlemen warriors of the clan as it had been. In came some of the same tacksmen as farmers in the new style. The reorganization meant fewer holdings and this meant that some of the tacksmen had to go. And go they did. They left for North America, and when it came to the Jacobite Rising of 1745 where were the tacksmen who would have formed the officer corps of Clan Campbell? They had in fair measure left.

In 1738, MacLeod of Dunvegan and MacDonald of Sleat arranged for some of their clansmen to be indentured and sent to the West Indies. It must be supposed that those two chiefs thought that they had a surplus of people on their estates and that they could turn necessity into profit by effectively selling their dependants into slavery. As the century passed, and particularly after the Forty-five, more and more of the relatively prosperous members of the clan society came to see that their chiefs no longer wanted them. The hardships of life in the Highlands were no longer compensated for by the tacksmen's social position, and they felt increasingly drawn to the idea of emigration to North America where, they thought, they would be able to re-create the conditions of their homeland without the incumbrance of oppressive chiefs. A Highland regiment (Fraser's Highlanders) was disbanded in North America at the end of the Seven Years War (1763), and the soldiers given land there on which to settle. News started to reach the Highlands that there was a better life across the Atlantic.

Emigration became an increasingly popular choice. Dr Johnson and James Boswell commented on it on their visit to the Hebrides in 1773 and, the following year, Flora MacDonald and her husband emigrated to North Carolina. Then, in the 1780s, there was the kelp boom.

Kelp was made by burning seaweed that had been cut from the great beds that grow off the shores of the West Highlands. It was a naturally produced forerunner of the soda that was manufactured from the early nineteenth century, and was used in the production of glass, soap and a number of other industrial processes. Expanding industry increased the demand for home-produced kelp, and then the onset of the continental wars increased it further. A lot of labour was necessary to produce kelp. People who had been put out of their farms by the arrival of sheep farming became a necessary labour force, and not an awkward surplus. The free granting of small parcels of ground, called crofts, encouraged people to marry young and the West Highlands entered a new phase of more rapid population growth. Kelpers could make a living cutting kelp and cultivating the crofts granted them by landowners. That, at least, was the idea. In practice the work was very hard and, although profitable for the landowners, left very little in the hands of kelpers.

West Highland landowners, who had noticed the increase in emigration without too much concern, now saw it as a threat to the successful commercial exploitation of their estates. They complained to the Government in the hope that legislation might be passed to hinder the emigrants, or at least the shipping agents who arranged their passage across the Atlantic. It is fair to say that some landowners were concerned at reports of the desperate conditions on board the emigrant ships and the great uncertainties that awaited emigrants on their arrival in North America.

The outbreak of war with France in 1793 encouraged the Government to recruit more Highland regiments for the British army. During the Seven Years War of the 1750s this had been easy. By the 1790s that was no longer the case. Many young men preferred to go to America. Many people in the Highlands remembered all too well the fate (death from diseases such as yellow fever) of so many Highland soldiers sent to the West Indies and to India. Recruitment became more difficult and the Government that had long relied on the Highlands as a source of manpower for the army and navy, became anxious. In 1803 the Passenger Vessels Act was passed. This made it more difficult to emigrate by introducing regulations to reduce overcrowding of vessels. Overtly the Act was philanthropic in intent, but the underlying intent was to make it more difficult to emigrate. It proved to be largely effective and exacerbated the problems resulting from over-population, chief of which was now the scarcity of cultivable land.

Up to about 1814 emigration had been mainly the recourse of relatively prosperous people in the Highlands. By the 1840s the effects of the most serious clearances made themselves felt in terms of congestion in the coastal townships, to which the people of the inland straths and glens had been driven. As the Potato Famine of that decade took its course landowners increasingly saw emigration as the only answer for many of the now destitute Gaels.

LOCH BROOM

Seen here from the Dirrie Mor, Loch Broom was the point of departure of many Highland emigrants from the middle of the eighteenth century. In 1746, after the failure of the Jacobite Rising at Culloden, the loch became the centre of attempts by the French to evacuate Prince Charles Edward. Eventually he was rescued from Loch nan Uamh, the place where he had landed just over a year earlier.

$\mathcal{S}$UTHERLAND

SUILVEN
The name is of Norse derivation and means Pillar Fell. The mountain's Gaelic name, Caisteal Liath (the Grey Castle), is preserved in the name of its main peak.

To the Gaels, Sutherland was Cataibh, the Land of the People of the Cat, while Caithness was Gallaibh, The Strangers' Country, because its fertile sandstone plain was a place of Norse settlement. The Norsemen of the eighth century called Sutherland so because it was the southern land, the first large chunk of mainland they reached as they sailed round Cape Wrath and down the Minch on their way to harry and settle the lands and islands down to the Isle of Man and Ireland. Names like Laxford (the Salmon Fjord) and the many names ending in 'dale' all the way down the west coast of the Highlands and the Western Isles are evidence of the Norse occupation which lasted from about AD 800 to 1266. For many Gaels, a large part of Sutherland, from the border of Caithness to Cape Wrath, was Duthaich Mhic Aoidh (MacKay's Country), and so it remains in the minds of many Scots throughout the world, even though the last of MacKay's Country was bought by the Dukes of Sutherland in 1829.

The Agricultural Revolution brought the white-faced sheep to the north and, by a curious irony, they are still at the heart of the rural economy despite being symbolic of so much misery in the past. Often now, particularly in the crofting world, sheep are one of the few remaining struts of the social framework. Shearing and dipping are activities that can need many hands and neighbours still find themselves helping each other at these events in the Northern and West Highlands. Visitors to Lairg can see the scale of the enterprise for themselves if they go to the first great annual sale in August, when it seems as though all the lambs of the northern glens are for sale through the mediation of those doyens of the business, United Auctions Ltd, formerly and more colourfully, Messrs Macdonald, Fraser of Perth.

THE FOUR-FOOTED CLANSMEN OF THE NORTH

Sheep and goats were among the first animals to be domesticated by humans and, up to medieval times, were probably more important in

A HIGHLAND CALF
Nowadays calves are sold after they have been weaned—at about one year old if born in the autumn, rather younger if spring-born—and may well be slaughtered at eighteen months. In the eighteenth century, however, they were kept by their breeder until they were between three and five years old.

the Highlands than cattle. The old Highland breed of sheep was rather small and much like the Shetland breed still found in those islands today. They were valued for the fine wool they produced, which was plucked rather than shorn from them, and for their milk and the cheese that could be made from it. The sheep were thought to be rather vulnerable and so were brought inside for the winter.

Black-face sheep arrived in the Southern Highlands in about 1760 and were a welcome addition to the already large farms of Argyll. Inexorably, the new sheep spread, reaching Sutherland in 1790. To start with they were very profitable for their owners, but overstocking and trade fluctuations brought a halt to the bonanza. By 1815 the great sheep fashion had run its course, although prices recovered periodically until about 1870, when refrigerated mutton from South America, Australia and New Zealand started to arrive in quantity in Britain.

The commonest breeds of sheep in the Highlands for the last 200 years have been the Scottish Black Face and the North Country Cheviot. The former are, in general, to be found throughout Perthshire, Argyll and Inverness-shire, while the North Country Cheviots are mainly in Sutherland and Wester Ross.

THE CLEARANCES

The Highland economy collapsed after the end of the Napoleonic Wars in 1815. Trade with the continent revived and prices for kelp dropped disastrously as overseas producers were able to supply the British market once more. Prices for wool, mutton and cattle fell and soldiers came home, paid off after the end of the war.

As the agricultural economy went into a state of crisis landowners realized that the growing numbers of people on their estates could not be sustained. The problems they faced were beyond their financial and administrative capacities. The only solution they could see was clearance followed by emigration.

In some parts of the Highlands, however, over-population did not trigger the clearance of the people. In these cases, of which the evictions of 1814 in Strathnaver and Kildonan are the best known, the clearances were often part of a programme of development and agricultural improvement. This is what happened on the Sutherland Estates.

DURNESS
Bright grass and a limestone wall indicate that Durness is an island of limestone country. It is a transformation from the surrounding wild and barren wastes of the lochans—peat and heather hummocks of the hard, acid Lewisian gneiss to the west and the monotonous country of the Moine schists to the east.

LOCH BRORA
Brora boasts a seam of high quality coal one metre (three and a quarter feet) thick and was the site of the only coal mine in the Highlands, closed some twenty years ago. The nearby Clynelish distillery once burned coal from the mine, but today uses oil in its place.

Briefly, the story is as follows: the Countess of Sutherland in her own right married the Marquess of Stafford, an English nobleman who had inherited an enormous fortune. Upon marrying his countess it seemed that investment in her vast estates in Sutherland would bring good returns, so a plan for the development of the estate was drawn up.

The plan envisaged the reorganization of the interior into holdings that were to be let to commercial sheep farmers. The people who occupied the existing grazings and lived in overcrowded poverty in such settlements as Rossal would be moved to the coast, where they would be allocated land for crofts (small-holdings). It was proposed that they would become fishermen and catch the herring that were plentiful off the northern and western coasts of Scotland at the time. Roads and harbours were to be built. In many ways the Sutherland Estate development plan was a model. It was carefully thought out, although in theoretical rather than practical terms, and backed by a large amount of capital. Moreover it had been specifically designed to benefit the people as well as the owners.

What went wrong? So far as the Gaels were concerned they had occupied the ground since time immemorial and had supported the Earls of Sutherland (and before that, in Strathnaver, the MacKays), either by service or by the payment of rent, or both. It seemed to the people that the Earls of Sutherland should look after their tenants just as they, the people, had maintained the Earls of Sutherland with their rents and their provision of men for the 93rd Highlanders during the Napoleonic Wars. The situation was not helped by a problem in communication. The representatives of the Marquess of Stafford and his lady did not speak Gaelic and made no effort to learn the language, while the people who were to be affected by the plan did not speak English (though probably no amount of explanation, however reasonably done, could have crossed the cultural barrier). Uncertain and miserable as their lot might sometimes be, it was preferable to the horror of banishment from the land of their ancestors. The logic of the landowners was incomprehensible to a society for whom co-operation and subsistence were the key to life and for whom economic competition was meaningless.

The Staffords' agents did not help matters by treating the Highlanders as idle savages and, to make matters worse, Patrick Sellar, one

STAC POLLAIDH
The slopes of Cul Beag run down from the left and those of Cul Mor from the right, framing Stac Pollaidh in the centre. The photograph was taken from near the Knockan Field Centre at the edge of the Cromalt Hills.

THE UPPER FALLS OF
RIVER CASSLEY *(overleaf)*
Autumn snow dusts the ground in Glen Cassley. A fragment of birch woodland turns from summer green through gold to rich brown.

of the senior employees of the Estate with responsibility for implementing the new plans, was to be the tenant of one of the new farms that was to be created out of the land. The people of Strathnaver could not fail to see that he was to be a beneficiary of their eviction.

Some evictions were carried out with great violence and little or no warning. Roofs were burned and, at Rossal, an old and sick woman evicted from her house died shortly afterwards. Sellar was tried for arson and culpable homicide for causing the death of this old lady, but was controversially acquitted. To this day the name of Patrick Sellar is execrated throughout the Highlands.

Then there was the question of the fishing. The Gaels, to the surprise of many who travelled among them, had never been great fishermen. They were pastoralists and farmers, and generally only fished for subsistence. They found themselves on the sea-shore without boats and without suitable skills. In addition, the herring that had been so plentiful during the late eighteenth century changed their pattern of migration and ceased to swim past the coast of Sutherland. There were, therefore, no herring to form the basis of the crofters' hypothetical prosperity as fishermen, even if they had been able to acquire boats.

Despite the bitterness that the first Clearances caused, large-scale evictions continued throughout the Highlands up to about 1880. Some were to clear land for sheep farming, others for the creation of deer forest. For the people, the episode of the Clearances confirmed finally that the role of the chiefs had changed irrevocably. They had become landowners for whom commercial interests had priority. For the Gaels, the betrayal was completed by the way in which Lowland Scots and Englishmen were usually preferred to Gaels as prospective tenants for the new farms.

THE HIGHLAND SPORTING ESTATE

The discovery of the Highlands by sportsmen, mainly from England, began in the late eighteenth century. It gathered momentum in the early nineteenth century with the publication of works such as Colonel Thornton's *Sporting Tour*, William Scrope's *The Art of Deer-stalking* and Charles St John's *Wild Sports of the Scottish Highlands*. To begin with the sportsmen enjoyed idyllic freedom, ranging over the hills

ROWAN AT INVERKIRKAIG
A view from Inverkirkaig across the Inverpolly National Nature Reserve. According to old lore, a brilliant show of rowan berries augurs a hard winter.

FISHING BOAT AT KINLOCHBERVIE
The 1970s were a time of optimism in the fishing industry of the North-west Highlands; generous grants were to be had from the Highland and Islands Development Board to buy new boats. Now many fishermen find themselves faced with large loans to pay back, restrictions on their fishing practices and the spectacle of foreigners fishing in what they regard as their waters.

shooting deer, grouse, black game and whatever else took their fancy. But in the course of time the landowners began to see the commercial possibilities of the shooting men, particularly after the fall in sheep prices that followed 1815, and things started to become more formal. Writing in 1843, my great-great-grandfather, Sir George Ramsay of Bamff wrote in his journal: '£1,200 yearly paid for Mar Lodge for the house and shooting. It would seem that the deer pay better than the sheep and cattle since Lord Fife's Trustees may be supposed to work to make the most of the property, for the benefit of the creditors. This the effect of competition among rich men from England. Cattle drive out men, now deer drive out cattle.'

The Highland sporting estate developed from this period. As sheep prices fluctuated throughout the nineteenth century and the burden of famine relief (particularly in the west) drained their resources, more Highland landowners were forced to sell their estates or to lease them for sporting purposes. Those that came on the market were bought eagerly. Some purchasers were from the traditional landed classes, while others had made fortunes in commerce and industry. The new railways eased earlier difficulties of transport. For these people the new estates were havens from the world of toil in the south. Their estates were holiday homes, where they might relax, shoot and fish. The lease of Balmoral by Queen Victoria in 1847, and its purchase in 1852 by the Prince Consort, set the seal on the fashion for a Highland home.

When the sheep were cleared off the new sporting estates it was often found that there were few red deer. Sometimes they colonized the cleared ground themselves. Sometimes they were imported from parks in England. At Rothiemurchus, which was first let as a deer forest in 1843, deer calves were brought over from Mar and released.

The new owners brought a degree of prosperity to the people on their estates. Shooting lodges were built. Elaborate water supplies, roads and bridges were constructed by members of a generation excited by the possibilities of applying new technologies. In spite of the relative prosperity that new owners brought to their estates and to those who worked for them, there was bitterness among many Gaels. Their betrayal in the previous century by their own chiefs turned landowners, and the misery induced by famine, clearance and emigration were compounded

HIGHLAND PONIES
Ponies have, for the most part, been replaced by rough terrain vehicles in their traditional role of removing the carcasses of deer from the hill. They are, however, still popular as riding ponies and for trekking.

DUN DORNAIGIL BROCH
Brochs such as this one in Sutherland were built on rocky ground near good soil and close to a supply of fresh water. They were built by warlords, people of considerable agricultural wealth, in the period 100BC to AD100.

STRATHCARRON, ARDGAY
A fringe of larch improves the appearance of a plantation of Sitka spruce, while birch grows on the little island in the loch.

by the attitudes of absolute and exclusive ownership of the land by these outsiders. Even in places like Morvern, where the new owners, the Smiths, brought greater material prosperity than had the Dukes of Argyll before them, their presence was still resented.

The sporting estates of the Highlands were never self-supporting economic units and even today they depend on income from outside. In Sutherland one may travel along the road from Durness down towards Loch Shin and, amid the wastes of the gloomy mountains of Moine schist, one comes upon an extraordinary settlement. This, with its crisply painted buildings and sheltering spruce trees, is the shooting lodge of a large estate. In its own terms this is a splendid place. It is well kept and employs a number of estate workers; deer stalkers, shepherds, gillies to help with the fishing, and some foresters. It has become a part of our Victorian heritage of land use. But it represents a form of land use, or range of land uses that is an end point. Climatic deterioration and human misuse, albeit committed in ignorance, have, in a marginal environment at a relatively high latitude, continued to impoverish the natural inheritance. To return suitable land to birch wood and so start the ecosystem on an upward path would be estimable.

PEATLAND AND AFFORESTATION

The change in climate about 7,000 years ago, bringing colder and wetter weather, reduced biological activity in the soil and so prevented soil organisms from decomposing the dead vegetation. Peat, the undecayed dead vegetation, started to form, and where there were ill-drained hollows in the land, it accumulated and the hollows became bogs. The bogs began to spread and the plants that had thrived in the warmer and drier phase found it more difficult to live and regenerate. The loss of the trees and, consequently, of their ability to move water from the soil into the atmosphere by the process of evapo-transpiration, contributed to the gradual waterlogging of the soil. In due course the peat covered the stumps and the dead trunks of the forests that had grown before.

With some variation, the climate that enabled the formation of peat has been with us ever since. In the peatlands of Caithness and Sutherland we have one of the most remarkable extents of this vegetational type in the world.

During the 1950s and 1960s work in the west of Ireland showed that trees from the western seaboard of Canada, Lodgepole pine and Sitka spruce, would grow on peat quite successfully and not blow over too soon. This encouraged the planting of areas previously thought to be unplantable and thus were added to the British forest land inventory many acres of apparently bare ground.

The forest cover of the British Isles reached an all-time low in the early years of this century, and the effect of the two World Wars was to make the Government aware of how little timber was produced at home. This led to tax incentives for landowners who replanted land that had been stripped during the wars and afforested more ground. When the implications of the tax incentives were realized, accountants and lawyers saw opportunities for clients. Thus the great British tax-efficient forestry operation was grafted on to the post-Second World War British forestry scene. Had the blanket Sitka mentality not been so excessive there would have been less objection. As it was some farmers benefited from the planting by others of sheltering woods that they could not have afforded to pay for themselves.

However, thousands of acres were afforested at great expense to the public with little possibility of any commercial return and the certainty of environmental damage.

For many, a great expanse of wet boggy landscape could be seen only as a waste to be put to use and consumed. Peat cut for fuel by a few crofters was not enough. Bogs had to be drained and turned to grass or into dreary plantations of exotic conifers that have failed until now even to bring the employment that their proposers claimed. This does not mean that there should be no new woods in Sutherland or elsewhere, only that we should learn from the existing native woods what we should be aiming to plant or regenerate. The message should be clear. We must be more ecologists and less engineers in our environment. Let us have less brutalist domination of the land.

In 1992 Scottish Natural Heritage put forward a Peatland Management Scheme in which it was proposed to pay landowners, tenant farmers and crofters for looking after peatlands. This scheme has now come into operation and with about one third of the eligible land covered by it so far included, may be so far judged to be a success.

CUL MOR

The Torridonian sandstone, from which Cul Mor is made, was formed almost 1,000 million years ago, initially from alluvial sediments dropped by the rivers of a continent that lay to the north-west of Scotland, into an ocean that long preceded the Atlantic. Sitting on a basement of the even more ancient Lewisian gneiss, the sandstone hills of the North-west Highlands are remnants of these deposits after many millions of years of erosion have done their work. Cul Mor is topped with a cap of white quartzite (about 500 million years old) as are several other hills in the region such as Liathach in Torridon and Suilven in Assynt.

BADENOCH AND STRATHSPEY

This bridge at Garvamore, built in 1731, is part of the military road linking the Perth-Inverness road at Dalwhinnie to Fort Augustus via the Corrieyairack Pass. It was constructed as part of the Government's programme to pacify the Highlands. Ironically, the Jacobite army under Prince Charles Edward crossed the pass in August 1745 by the very road that had been built to forestall such a possibility.

BADENOCH MEANS the Drowned Land and includes the parishes of Laggan, Kingussie and Insh, Alvie, Duthil, Rothiemurchus and Kincardine on Spey. It stretches west beyond Loch Laggan to border Lochaber. Badenoch is the crossroads of the Highlands.

Strathspey is less easily defined, but is often taken to include the country between the two Craigellachies on the River Spey. The upper Craigellachie is just to the west of Aviemore and looks over it from within its National Nature Reserve of birch wood. At the lower Craigellachie, Thomas Telford's iron bridge spans the Spey. A large part of the Cairngorm massif lies within Badenoch and Strathspey, but that is described in the next chapter.

The influence of the River Spey, rising far back in Monadhliath, pervades this land of forest, wetland and loch. Stock farms are located in the clearings and, as one penetrates to the higher ground of Badenoch, west of the A9, they give way to hill sheep farms and deer forests.

The River Spey is famous for its salmon fishing and so, faced with an invidious choice in a land so rich with rivers known for their fishing, I have chosen to write about salmon in this chapter. Further on there are pieces about the pine woods of Speyside and the capercaillie. Reminding myself of the Laird of Rothiemurchus's famous present of whisky to King George IV in 1822, I have included that pleasant topic in this chapter as well.

THE ATLANTIC SALMON – A KING IN PERIL

From the autumn through to January and even February, Atlantic salmon (*Salmo salar*) spawn in the rivers where they started life some years before. They spawn wherever the gravel and hydrodynamics are suitable, from source to mouth—and certainly in much of the main river. The female fish makes a hollow in a gravelly patch. She achieves

GARVAMORE
A wintry scene in upper Strathspey near Garvamore. The upper plain of Spey has been subject to flooding since earliest times and the name Badenoch means the 'drowned land'. Despite the building of embankments at Garvamore and canalization at Insh there is still periodic flooding.

this without touching the gravel, which is lifted by the hydraulic effect of the lateral flexing of her body and swept downstream by the current. Then she is joined by a male. Lying alongside each other, they extrude their eggs and sperm together. Afterwards, the cock moves away and the hen fish, having moved slightly upstream, starts to make another redd, thus filling the previous one, in which the fertilized eggs lie. Finally, she fills in the top redd.

Salmon do not feed while they are in fresh water and having mated they are spent. In short rivers such as the Laxford, they survive, but in long rivers such as the Spey most die as they swim back down the river, although a few, particularly females, survive and reach the sea.

The fertilized eggs hatch towards the end of March. Eventually the young fish make their way through the gravel that covers them and for the next two or three years they stay in the river of their birth, growing and developing. During this time they are described as fry, parr and smolt as they pass through different phases of growth. At the smolt stage, when the fish are between two and three years old and about 11–15 centimetres (4½–6 inches) long, they set off for the sea. Leaving fresh water in late March, April, or May, most smolts make for the deep waters of the Atlantic off Greenland, where they stay for a year or more. At this stage many are caught by the Greenlanders' shore and drift nets. Some probably do not go as far as Greenland and return to the river of their birth as grilse, that is to say having spent only one winter at sea. These fish seem to feed north of the Faeroes and some are caught on the long lines of the Faeroese fishermen. Most salmon, however, reach the waters around Greenland and eventually come back to Scotland as two sea-winter fish.

Not all salmon return to all the rivers at the same time. Some rivers are known as spring-run rivers because most of the salmon come back then, while others are called autumn-run rivers for that reason. Yet other waters have salmon returning from spring through to the autumn. The reappearance of salmon in the rivers where they spawned has always been a matter of amazement. It is known now, however, that salmon are guided back to their rivers of origin by a sense of smell. The water of each river has a unique chemical composition and it seems that it is to this that the salmon are receptive.

SHEEP ON GARVAMORE
Round balers were introduced in the 1970s and made mechanical feeding of sheep possible. A tractor's fore-end loader can pick up a bale and, after cutting the string, the bale can be placed in the ring feeder and left for the sheep. There is however a cost. When fed in ring feeders, round bales of hay can cause extensive poaching of the land and, where these feeders are used on moorland, this destroys the heather.

As they enter fresh water salmon start to lose the sea lice that they have picked up on their journey and they begin the fast that will continue until they have reached the spawning beds, or died.

At the mouths of the rivers inshore nets are set and lifted according to old rules. Then there are the fishermen, with rod and line, and the poachers, some of them using cyanide gas. There are the obstacles of the hydro-electric schemes, the pollution of fresh waters by pesticide residues from sheep dips, and farm effluents such as those produced by silage. The impacts of fish farming are already adding to the many hazards that salmon face, but the most important factor affecting the reproductive success of salmon is probably the loss, or deterioration, of spawning and nursery areas. Some of this loss is due to ill-advised schemes to straighten rivers with the intention of reducing flooding in winter. The flooding itself is made worse by the drainage of uplands for forestry and of bogs for agriculture.

NATIVE PINEWOODS, THE BOREAL EDGE

The native pine woods of Speyside are fragments of the huge forest that covered much of the North-eastern Highlands 7,000 years ago. The Nature Conservancy Council's *Nature Conservation Review* of 1977 makes this clear in treating as one entry the pine woods from Glen Tanar, Ballochbuie, Glen Derry and Glen Quoich on Deeside, and those of Rothiemurchus, Glen More and Abernethy on the north side of the Cairngorms massif. As elsewhere there is evidence of very early interaction between humans and trees. Archaeologists have found traces of cultivation by Neolithic farmers in the soil on which the pine woods of Loch Garten now grow, and there is evidence that the shores of Loch Pityoulish were cleared of forest 3,000 years ago.

In spite of deforestation, the pine woods of the Central and Eastern Highlands show a capacity for regeneration whenever they are given the chance. This is particularly evident in parts of Deeside, as on Creagan Riach and Crannach Hill above Ballater. It would be the case even in the woods at Glen Derry and Glen Quoich above Braemar, but management of the estate of Mar Lodge as a deer forest since the 1760s (a return to its medieval use) has resulted in the failure of young trees to grow since the late eighteenth century. None of the pines there is less

GLENMORE FOREST PARK
Glenmore was let as a sheep walk in the early nineteenth century and then, in 1923, the Duke of Richmond and Gordon sold it to the Forestry Commission, who declared it a National Forest Park in 1948. Unfortunately, much of the magnificent pine forest was felled and exotic conifers planted in its place. In recent years, however, the Forestry Commission have started to cut out the exotics and to encourage the regeneration of the native forest. Scenes such as this, with old 'Granny' pines and their descendants thriving together, are becoming more common.

LOCH MORLICH
Late winter in Strathspey and the snowy Cairngorms rise behind the Glenmore Forest Park. The loch has become a centre for boating and recreation.

than about 200 years old, but they continue to produce viable seed. Seedlings proliferate only to be eaten by red deer as they appear above the heather. The magnificent woods at Rothiemurchus show a wonderful profusion of regeneration around Loch an Eilein. They give an idea of how the derelict Braemar woods and the battered Glen Feshie woods on the west side of the Cairngorms could look if only proper attention were given to their management.

If failure to regenerate in the drier Eastern Highlands is primarily due to overgrazing, the reasons for failure are not so clear in the West and Northern Highlands. The damper oceanic climate of the region, often leading to waterlogging and subtle changes in the soils, like those in the mycorrhizal flora, may provide part of the answer. In addition, the activities of voles, shrews and deer may have altered in importance or intensity since the eighth millenium before present. The climate itself has changed over the millennia.

One of our problems in trying to understand forests and their ecology is that we often imprison the woods inside fences and so restrict their capacity to regenerate and develop. Birch and pinewoods can be surprisingly mobile in natural conditions.

The activities of humans, including grazing by domestic livestock as well as deer, have been shown to limit the development of diversity. They have made the birch less common in many pinewoods than it was and this may well have influenced the life of the pinewood. Birch is an important component of the pinewood community as a pioneering species, improving the quality of the soil. It has been suggested that the presence of birch in pinewoods may improve the resistance of the woods to wind-blow. Experimental exclosures in the Black Wood of Rannoch have shown dramatic resurgence of rowan.

The importance of the native pine woods of the Highlands is manifold. From a bio-geographical point of view they are the western edge of the Great Boreal Forest belt of the Eurasian land mass. As such they have a contribution to make to global bio-diversity in the genetic distinctiveness of the pines themselves and their uniqueness as a forest ecosystem. As a restored part of this increasingly threatened forest belt they have potentially a part to play in climatic regulation (the dark canopies of the trees absorbing heat from the sun and so warming the

STRATHSPEY ABOVE NEWTONMORE
This area was home to James Macpherson who was born in nearby Kingussie in 1736 and became a school master at Ruthven. In 1760 he produced for an astonished and receptive public what he claimed were the writings of a Gaelic poet called Ossian. In spite of the subsequent bitter controversy, in which it was suggested that Macpherson himself was the author, the poems helped fire the Romantic Movement, the Celtic Revival and much else, and were read widely by a public which included Napoleon and Goethe.

forest, especially in the winter), a significant consideration in a period of climatic instability. They also play an important role in the regulation of the hydrological cycle, slowing down the speed with which flood waters make their way to the large rivers and so to the sea, but improving flow in times of drought. The native forest can never banish flooding, but it can diminish it by increasing the time it takes for a flood to reach its peak, and so reduce the damage that may be done to farmland down in the flood plain.

Another important part played by the forest is the protection of soil from accelerated erosion. The tree canopy of the forest intercepts rain drops as they fall, reducing their impact on the ground and so slowing soil erosion. At a local level, woods moderate climatic extremes, providing shelter from the wind and mitigating the effects of rain and snow in winter, while in summer the cool shade of the woods refreshes the visitor.

As if all this were not enough, native woodland is, if managed properly, a valuable and self renewing resource for timber and a spectacle of triumphant beauty. The pinewoods are the habitats of a range of animals and plants that are dependent on them. Characteristic birds of the pinewoods are the Scottish crossbill and the crested tit, but perhaps the best known is the capercaillie, whose name probably comes from the Gaelic *capullcoille*, meaning horse of the wood. The bird's continued survival is closely bound up with the health and extent of the pinewoods on which it depends. Since the 1970s the numbers of capercaillie appear to have been in decline and further destruction of its habitat will put its status in Scotland in jeopardy.

THE RISE OF WHISKY

Although whisky was drunk in the Highlands before the eighteenth century, it had not won the universal popularity that it now has. Edmund Burt, the engineer officer whose letters from the Highlands to a friend in England tell us so much about life in the Highlands before the middle of that century, certainly refers to whisky often enough, but Thomas Pennant, the naturalist, describes it as a new drink in the 1770s. Up to that time it seems that beer was the beverage of the ordinary folk, while the chiefs and gentry drank wine, particularly

LOCH AN EILEIN
Rothiemurchus was at one time a Comyns stronghold and it is thought that the Castle of Loch an Eilein was one of theirs. After the fall of the Comyns in 1314, Rothiemurchus was acquired by the Shaws and it was then sold on to the Grants, who still own it, in about 1580.

INSH MARSHES

The reed beds, wet meadows, herb-rich swamp and willow carr of the Insh marshes are important breeding places and winter feeding grounds for a number of species of water birds. These include the golden eye, spotted crake and the wood sandpiper. In winter, flocks of whooper swans feed in the marshes and hen-harriers roost among the reed beds.

claret (exempt from duty until about 1780), and brandy or rum for preference. There was also an *aqua vitae*, which was distilled from the roots of certain plants and flavoured with herbs, while gin was popular in the Lowlands.

The great change in drinking preferences was due, in part, to the introduction of the potato in the 1750s. Its enormous productivity meant that ground could be released from growing barley for food and devoted to the production of malt, to make whisky. Whisky was valuable because it could be used instead of money as a currency for paying rent; a currency, moreover, that did not spoil readily, and kept its value. Above all, distilling whisky was profitable and this meant that tenants were able to pay their rents. Naturally this appealed to both landowners and tenants, although some lairds thought that tenants who made whisky had less time for their farms and were more inclined to be dissolute than those who confined themselves to farming.

The wars with France and the imposition of heavy excise duties from the 1780s made wine and brandy harder to come by, despite the efforts of smugglers. Gradually, whisky replaced them.

The impossibility of enforcing absurd laws about the licensing of stills and the taxation of barley and malt ensured a flourishing underground industry and much smuggling, particularly to the Lowlands, where the duty on whisky was heavier than in the Highlands. By the early nineteenth century a great deal of whisky was being drunk throughout Scotland. In her *Letters from the Highlands*, Elizabeth Grant of Rothiemurchus describes how whisky was drunk at every possible moment and how George IV himself, on his visit to Edinburgh in 1822, was treated to illicit Glenlivet whisky, a gift from her father, Grant of Rothiemurchus. The connivance of so many, from the highest to the lowest in the land, made a mockery of the law and it was changed in 1824. The excise duty was lowered to a point where it made better sense for bigger producers to pay the tax than try avoiding it. However, it also had the effect of putting smaller distillers out of business and this contributed to the misery of the emerging crofting community of the 1830s and 1840s. None the less, the legislation of 1824 set the foundations for the development of the Scotch whisky industry as we know it to this day.

RUTHVEN BARRACKS

The site of the barracks, built after 1719 as a result of the 1715 Rising and later disturbances, is a natural mound which had already been the site of one of the ubiquitous Comyn castles. All that survives of the earlier building is the well. It was here that Jacobite troops met after the Battle Culloden, expecting to find the Prince and receive further orders. The Prince, however, had already made for the west.

THE CAIRNGORMS AND THE EASTERN HIGHLANDS

BESIDE THE DEE

The Dee is one of the famous salmon rivers of Scotland. The river's name itself derives from the Gaulish word for Goddess.

CAIRNGORM (CARN GORM means the blue or green cairn) is the name of a mountain which is 1,245 metres (4,084 feet) high. It has given its name to the range which has been described as 'the largest and most important mountain system in the British Isles'. The range was known to the Gaels as Monadh Ruadh, meaning the Red Mountain Range, due to its underlying red granite.

There is more land above 1,200 metres (*c.* 4,000 feet) in the Cairngorms than in any other part of the British Isles (four of Scotland's five highest mountains are in the range). The Cairngorms National Nature Reserve covers some 63,000 acres (25,200 hectares)of this high plateau which, with its dramatic, deep corries and lochs, its arctic to sub-arctic climate and montane vegetation and fauna, has been described as a slab of the Arctic 1,000 miles (1,610 kilometres) too far south. The River Dee rises in the heart of the range at 1,309 metres (4,300 feet), the greatest fall from source to sea of any river in the British Isles.

The remoteness of this high country meant that, until recently, it was hardly affected by humans and their activities. It was a wilderness in a way that little other countryside in the British Isles has been for many hundreds of years.

In recent years, the enormous increase in recreation has brought pressures to the Cairngorms. Skiing, and its associated chairlifts, has enabled large numbers of people to reach the fragile ecosystems of the plateau. Litter left on the skiing slopes has resulted in greater numbers of crows and other opportunist species such as herring gulls. This has potentially damaging consequences for ground-breeding birds of the high plateau like the dotterel. Erosion of slopes has resulted from the compaction of snow by skiing.

Further afield, estates have bulldozed tracks into the hills, as in upper Glen Feshie, in order to transport shooting clients nearer to the red grouse or the red deer. Increased access of this kind is exposing this area to degradation. Failure to manage the numbers of red deer and sheep has led to overgrazing and has been the most important factor in the inability of woods to regenerate. Commercial afforestation has also had a damaging environmental impact, as has the acidification of the lochs due to acid rain.

The question of how to take care of the Cairngorms is not a new one. In 1945 the Scottish National Parks Survey Committee recommended that the area should become a national park. Regrettably, the Government of the day turned the proposal down.

In 1987 the Countryside Commission for Scotland and the Nature Conservancy Council proposed to the Scottish Office that the Cairngorms should be proposed to UNESCO as a World Heritage Site. The Scottish Office accepted this recommendation, but it quickly became apparent that the area was likely to be turned down for this accolade because of the failure to safeguard it adequately. A working party was set up to discuss the future of the Cairngorms and to consider how best the area might be managed. Its report, published in December 1992, recommended that the core of the Cairngorms and a wide zone that would include much of the Eastern Highlands should become a Natural Heritage Area.

The Eastern Highlands are above all an area of heather moorland, deer forest and sheep farms and Deeside is particularly remarkable for the extent of its pine and birch forest. The country is criss-crossed with paths and old routes such as Jock's road, that goes from the head of Glen Doll over to Deeside by way of Glen Callater, and the famous path through Glen Tilt in Atholl that crosses to Braemar.

HEATHER MOORLAND

The heather moorlands of the Eastern Highlands have, for many people, come to symbolize Scotland. They are dominated by the ling (*Calluna vulgaris*), whose little purple flowers colour the hills. A number of associated species make up the plant community, including cross-leaved heath (*Erica tetralix*), bell heather (*Erica cinerea*), blaeberry

BIRCHWOOD ABOVE BRAEMAR
The slopes of the hills around Braemar are clothed with birchwood. The foreground shows old, declining trees and a woodland floor that is heavily grazed. Grazing pressure apart, birch does not regenerate well in the shade of older trees. Research in 1986 showed that the area of birch woodland on Deeside had stayed much the same for the past fifty years, but only because new areas of colonization had made up for areas of decline and loss.

CORGARFF CASTLE
Corgarff was manned by Government troops during the eighteenth century as part of the subjugation of the Highlands. The eighteenth-century outworks incorporated developments in military engineering. They enabled defending troops to give covering fire to other parts of the fortification that might be under attack. Behind the castle lies a moorland that is managed for grouse shooting. The heather is burned in small patches to provide a range of habitat for grouse.

(*Vaccinium myrtillus*), crowberry (*Vaccinium vitis-idaea*), and bear-berry (*Arctostaphylos uva-ursi*). Several species of mosses and lichens are also important constituents of the moorland ecosystem. The vegetation of these heaths is characteristically patterned like a mosaic.

Heaths flourish on rather acidic soils and are most abundant in the drier east side of the country, although they do also grow in the west. The Isle of Lewis, for example, is known as Eilean Fraoich (The Island of Heather).

Most heather moorland, as we know it in the British Isles, is the result of human intervention. The earliest clearance of forest by the Neolithic farmers resulted in the spread of moorland beyond its primaeval range north of the forest in the sub-arctic region, and above the tree line. To some extent this may have coincided with climatic changes that favoured its development rather than that of woodland.

The expansion of the Highland cattle trade in the eighteenth century, growth of the human population, and the change to extensive sheep production continued to favour the spread of moorland. In addition, the use of fire in the management of moorland for pasture ensured that the woods could not regenerate. The spread of open heather moorland provided more habitat for red grouse and was responsible for the increase in their numbers. When sheep prices collapsed in the early nineteenth century, the artificially large numbers of birds had already attracted the sporting man's attention. From this time the management of heather moorland for grouse shooting developed as a form of land use in the Highlands.

The enemies of heather are overgrazing by sheep and increasingly by red deer, and too much burning. Heather is not an especially competitive plant and, if burning is too severe, grasses and bracken invade and take over, as has happened over large areas of the Highlands, particularly in the west. As a consequence much heathland has disappeared in recent years. Apart from the causes listed above, much has also been lost to afforestation and some to the reseeding of land with grass for agricultural purposes.

The loss of heathland in Europe has made the heather moorlands of the British Isles important for the whole continent as the habitat of a number of species of birds. It supports not only grouse, but merlins,

BRAEMAR CASTLE
In August 1715 the Earl of Mar, having changed his coat in more ways than one, embarked secretly in London on a ship bound for Scotland. On his arrival at Braemar, he summoned the other chiefs of the country under the guise of a deer hunt and raised the Royal Standard of the Stewarts.

peregrine falcons, hen harriers, golden eagles, short-eared owls and a range of wading birds, including golden plovers, lapwing, curlew, and redshank.

THE FATE OF THE GROUSE

It used to be thought that the red grouse (*Lagopus lagopus scoticus*) was unique to the British Isles, but now it is considered to be of the same species as the European willow grouse, although belonging to a different sub-species. The fact that the red grouse belongs to a species that, in its main European range, favours the forest edge, tells us something about the bird and its ancient habitat. In Scotland it belongs predominantly to the heather moors, but without deforestation the bird would be, like its continental relations, an inhabitant of the heathery edge of the pine forests and their clearings.

The ecology of the red grouse has been the subject of much research because of its value as a game bird. Grouse are strongly territorial and their year goes like this. In the autumn, the cocks choose their territories for the following season and start to pair. Any birds that fail to find a territory are eventually expelled from the core area of heather moorland and have to find less favourable sites. Where there are enough of these territory-less birds they fly about in packs and often frequent the country at the edge of the moor, which is less heathery and less strongly defended. Most of these birds die during the winter, either through starvation or predation. Mortality among birds that hold territories, and their mates, is generally low. Such as occurs is due mainly to predation. If territory-holding birds or their mates die, they are replaced by non-territorial birds. During May the birds mate and the hen lays a clutch of six to twelve eggs on the ground. The chicks hatch later that month and grow through the summer, before reaching mature size in August. Red grouse chicks eat insects for the first week or two of their lives, but thereafter feed largely on heather, like adult birds.

Grouse shooting began in the late eighteenth century when firearms had become light enough and sufficiently reliable for the purpose. Initially the birds were shot on the ground. Dogs were trained to point to the place where the concealed grouse was hiding and the shooter could look for the bird and shoot it when he saw it. As weapons and

GROUSE MOOR IN STRATHDON
It is well-known that grouse numbers fluctuate, but they have also been tending to fall in recent decades, and it is clear that habitat decline has been the main cause. Heavy grazing by sheep and red deer favours the growth of grass at the expense of heather—the grouse's favoured habitat.

BRAEMAR VILLAGE
*Once called the Castleton of
Braemar, the village became a centre
of tourism for Upper Deeside and
was the rail head of the now defunct
Deeside line. In recent times the
people of Upper Deeside have been
Highland in speech, although the last
native Gaelic speakers here died
about twenty years ago.*

ammunition improved it became possible for the birds to be shot while on the wing. The practice of shooting the birds changed to one of using the dogs to point or set the birds, which, on becoming airborne, would be shot at. This kind of shooting was relatively informal and became extremely popular. Indeed its popularity came as an enormous relief to Highland landowners in the years of poor sheep prices which followed the end of the Napoleonic Wars, and in other, later years of agricultural depression.

The practice of driving grouse is said to have originated in the 1880s when the Prince of Wales, Queen Victoria's son, and later Edward VII, decided that he would like to have the grouse driven to him by groups of men walking towards the shooters in a line, rather than having to walk all over a moor looking for them.

The introduction of shooting grouse in this way coincided with the heyday of the shooting estate and, possibly by coincidence, with a peak in the grouse population. By the First World War (1914-18) the annual grouse bags of many estates had declined and such was the anxiety among owners of grouse moors that a commission was set up under the chairmanship of the then Lord Lovat to look into the problem. Lord Lovat's report, *The Grouse in Health and in Disease*, was published in 1911, and gave research into grouse a base line. The report was much studied and discussed by those interested in the subject. Considerable emphasis in the report was placed on the infestation of grouse populations by the parasitic worm *Strongylus*. During the 1930s the numbers of grouse being shot had once more reached levels that moor owners considered satisfactory, and then the Second World War intervened. By the late forties and early fifties the owners of Highland estates were once again worried by a drop in their bags of grouse.

Under the auspices of the state conservation service (the newly established Nature Conservancy), the Department of Zoology of Aberdeen University, and with initial funding from the Scottish Landowners' Federation, a long term project was set up to study the ecology of the red grouse.

One of the resulting developments was the concept of the 'doomed surplus', an idea which population ecologists had evolved in their attempts to understand the complex population dynamics of animals.

It implied that the consequences of winter predation, particularly by birds of prey like the peregrine falcon or the golden eagle, might be insignificant for the shootable population of the coming season.

Another question that arose was that within the overall apparent decline in the numbers of grouse, there appeared to be ups and downs which looked like cycles. If this was happening then why? By the 1980s the researchers, working by now for the Institute of Terrestrial Ecology, were willing to predict ups and downs in the cycle with some success.

RED DEER AND THEIR CONSERVATION

In 1970 there were about 180,000 red deer in Scotland; by 1991 there were estimated to be some 320,000. In 1954, when the Cairngorms National Nature Reserve was established, there were thought to be too many red deer in the area and they were seen to be preventing the regeneration of the old woods. What has brought about this increase? Two words sum up the background to the changes—climate and management. In summer there is enough grazing for deer and sheep on the hills. However, in late winter (from March to May), good forage becomes scarce and this is above all the time when red deer starve, particularly in years when the snow lies late or the weather is wet and windy. The winters of the late 1980s were mild; the snow melted early and more deer were able to survive the winters. These facts of climate have been associated with the recent increase of the red deer population, which has been particularly marked in the Eastern Highlands. Before that, however, insufficient culling was the most important factor in excessive deer numbers. Along with red deer, the most important grazers of the hills are sheep. The number of sheep kept in the hills depends on the profitability of sheep-farming and this depends on the amount of support the industry is given by the European Community through the Common Agricultural Policy. Red deer and, in particular, hinds do not like to share their grazing with sheep (as Donnchadh Ban Macintyre noticed in the eighteenth century), because they compete for the forage, but also for other reasons that are not yet fully understood. The interaction between sheep and deer on the hills is part of the background to the increase in deer numbers. Afforestation with conifers of areas that were the traditional wintering grounds for stags has added to

UPLAND SHEEP AT STRATHDON
Tupping time on a farm in Strathdon. A flock of ewes runs with a Cheviot ram. The latter is rather out of breath after nearly a year of idleness since his services were last called upon.

the problem. The fencing of these areas against them has meant that stags have been forced to look for new wintering grounds. With the passage of time, however, fences often cease to be effective and the plantations become accessible to the deer, first as shelter, then as permanently occupied ground with a breeding population of stags and hinds. Controlling deer in these thick plantations is extremely difficult and counting them almost impossible. The red deer of the plantations have become an important part of the problem. As a rule the managers of deer forests have been inclined to shoot too few hinds in relation to the number of stags they cull (though this is changing). As one stag can serve a large number of hinds this has the effect of setting in progress a rapid increase in the numbers of red deer. But why have deer managers been shooting too few hinds? Historically, they have wanted to keep many hinds on their ground in the belief that this would attract plenty of stags. Shooters prefer to stalk (or hunt) stags rather than hinds because, apart from their more impressive size, stags' antlers are greatly valued as trophies. Estates can, therefore, charge considerably more for the shooting of stags.

Another important consideration is that the season for shooting stags lasts from 11 August to 20 October. Hinds, on the other hand, are not shot until after 20 October and their season does not end until the beginning of February. This means that much of the time when hinds may be shot coincides with the harsh winter weather, making it far more difficult to carry out an efficient cull. As stags represent their most valuable form of revenue many estates feed them through the hardest part of the winter to keep as many as they can on their ground. The managers of the estates hope that the deer will not wander off to lower ground and risk being shot by farmers, trying to save the turnips that they have grown for their sheep and cattle, or by foresters intent on keeping them out of their woods. This means that deer forests where stags are fed (hinds are less inclined to come in to feed) may carry an artificially large number of stags through the period which, in a truly natural situation, would be the survival bottle neck when many would die.

On top of this many estates have fertilized, limed and reseeded wintering pastures, and others have opened fields that were part of farms to deer, fuelling further increase in their numbers.

RED DEER
Red deer are herd animals and groups occupy a home range. The hinds form the basic range holding group of the red deer and companies of stags occupy a different part of the hill for most of the year. The rut is in the autumn; from the end of September to the end of October. This is the time for individual stags to try to herd groups of hinds and mate with them. Other stags without hinds challenge those that have harems. Sometimes they manage to replace such a stag after fighting with him. This stag and his hinds are grazing in the neighbourhood of Braemar.

A PLANTATION OF PINES *(overleaf)*
The bare woodland floor of this plantation by the side of the road to Inverey contrasts sharply with the healthy shrub-rich woods found by Loch an Eilein in Rothiemurchus, or the woods at Abernathy in Strathspey. Grazing by too many red deer is the cause.

THE LAIRIG GHRU
On the horizon is the Bod an Diabhoil (Devil's Point) and further on Cairntoul (carn an t-sabhail means the cairn of the barn).

So estates have been feeding to maintain too many stags, but also have too many hinds producing calves. How many are too many? It depends on who you are. For the conservationist and the farmer there are too many deer when the heather is so overgrazed that it cannot regenerate, and other forms of herbage, particularly grasses like the robust and un-nutritious mat-grass (*Nardus stricta*) spread on to ground formerly occupied by heather and by the more nourishing bent-fescue grasses. For the conservationist (and forester) there are too many deer when woodland in the deer forest cannot regenerate. This is the case in many places and in particular in the remaining native pine woods of Mar, where too much grazing by red deer for the last two centuries has left woods that are shells, with old trees but no young ones. For Scottish Natural Heritage, charged with the conservation of habitat types, like the birch wood at Creag Meagaidh in Badenoch, it is necessary to carry out severe culls of the red deer in order to prevent the deer destroying the woods which are part of the National Nature Reserve. Research carried out there by SNH is showing that reductions in the numbers of deer can be made without affecting the deer stocks of neighbouring estates adversely. Deer management groups, like that in the East Grampians, are now making serious attempts to come to grips with the problem of too many red deer in their area by greatly increasing the hind culls. Many deer forest owners have regarded abundance of red deer as important for itself, and so it is questionable whether the definition of over-grazing that I have given applies. Indeed, it may seem like a recipe for financial disaster. How is a living to be made if the deer are to be reduced to numbers that will allow natural regeneration of trees to take place? This is the nub of the problem. However, deer forest owners are increasingly prepared to accept that fewer deer may mean heavier deer and thus stags bearing finer antlers, resulting in equally good financial returns from fewer deer shot.

It is clear that the ecological balance has been very much disturbed. Long ago there were wolves and lynxes as well as humans to prey upon the red deer and maintain their numbers within the limits imposed by climate and habitat. Red deer are part of the ecosystem of the woods; at low and moderate densities they contribute to the process of natural regeneration of the forest, but at high densities they destroy it. Unless

THE LAIRIG GHRU
The pass through the Lairig Gru (Lairig means pass) runs beside the River Dee, which rises 2,000 feet (600 metres) to the summit plateau of Braeriach and leads over to Strathspey through the heart of the Cairngorms.

the process of degradation of the Highlands is to continue indefinitely we shall have to find a way of managing red deer as a part of that ecosystem.

FHIR A SHIUBHLAS AM BEALACH

There has always been a tendency to marry the girl or boy next door. No doubt this was also true for the Highlands in days gone by, but then as now it was sometimes necessary to go courting further afield. As they undertook long journeys on foot to visit their sweethearts, the Highlanders of old had plenty of time to consider the land they walked through; to notice the flight of birds, the footprints of animals, the way the wind blew.

In 1687 Rob Roy MacGregor's brother, Iain, married Christian Campbell of Duneaves, near Fortingall at the foot of Glenlyon. In order to visit her, Iain must have walked about thirty miles (fifty kilometres)—unless he sailed or rowed along Loch Tay). He got his girl so he was lucky, as was Finlay, father of Domhnall MacFhionnlaidh nan Dan, who had only to cross Rannoch Moor to reach Loch Treig in Lochaber to get to his sweetheart. Finlay may have been at one of the Glencoe peoples' shielings looking after cattle, while his wife-to-be was at one of the Keppoch shielings on the other side of the moor. For others, however, this long-distance courting cannot have been so easy. Several songs contain lines like these, composed early in the nineteenth century by a drover from Loch Alsh: '*Fhir a shiùbhlas a null thar bhealaichean, Thoir soraidh bhuam-sa a dh'ionnsaigh Ealasaid.*' ('You who travel yonder across the passes, Take a greeting from me to Elizabeth.') Another young man who clearly had difficulties with distance, made worse by a tricky employer (not to speak of the possibility that he was already married to someone else) was the shepherd in Drumochter:

> *Gu'm bheil mulad air m'intinn*
> *Bho'n a thànaig mi'n tìr seo,*
> *'S nach fhaic mi mo nighneag dhonn, òg.*
> *Bho nach fhaic mi mo chaileag*
> *Do'n d'thug mi 'n gaol falaich—*
> *'S ann a dh'fhàg mi i 'n Raineach nam bo.*

SPITAL OF GLEN SHEE
Glen Shee has been an important route through the Eastern Highlands since time immemorial. Medieval kings travelled through the glen on their way to hunt in the Forest of Mar, probably stopping for the night at the Spital on their way there. The word Spital means hospice; this one was kept by the Cistercian monks of Coupar Angus to shelter travellers. Now the Spital is a centre for the skiing industry, whose slopes are beyond the Devil's Elbow at the top of nearby Gleann Beag.

1542–67	Mary I.
c.1550	Start of the Little Ice Age (lasts 200 years).
1567–1625	James VI.
1585	Marriage of King James VI to Anne of Denmark.
1603	Death of Elizabeth I of England and Union of the Crowns of Scotland and England.
1609	Statutes of Iona.
1625–49	Charles I.
1645	Battle of Inverlochy.
1649–85	Charles II.
1651–8	The Rule of Cromwell in England.
1652	Defeat of Royalist Army at Battle of Worcester and subsequent invasion of Scotland and rule of Scotland by Cromwell until 1658.
1685–8	James VII (and II of England).
1689–94	William 'III' and Mary 'II'.
1689	The Revolution—Battle of Killiecrankie.
1690s	Famine—King William's 'lean years'.
1692	Massacre of Glencoe.
1694–1702	William 'III'.
1698	Darien Expedition.
1702–14	Anne.
1707	Union of Parliaments.
1715	Jacobite Rising.
1719	The Affair of Glenshiel.
1739	Embodiment of The Black Watch.
1745–6	Jacobite Rising.
1746	Battle of Culloden. The Disarming Act.
1752	Appin Murder.
1756–63	Seven Years War.
1760	Accession of George III.
1771	Birth of Sir Walter Scott.
1773	Voyage of the *Hector* from Loch Broom.
1782	The repeal of the Disarming Act.
1783	Famine.
1788	Death of Prince Charles Edward Stuart in Rome.
1793	Outbreak of Revolutionary War with France.
1814	Clearances in Strathnaver. Publication of *Waverley* by Sir Walter Scott.
1815	End of Napoleonic Wars. Fall in sheep prices. Collapse of kelp industry.
1822	George IV's visit to Edinburgh. The opening of the Caledonian Canal.
1840s	Famine.
1870–80s	Slump in agricultural prices.
1882	The Crofters' War.
1883	Napier Commission.
1886	Crofters' Holding Acts.
1943	Establishment of the North of Scotland Hydro-Electric Board.

BIBLIOGRAPHY

G. W. S. Barrow, *The Kingdom of the Scots*; *Kingship and Unity*; *Robert Bruce and the Community of the Realm of Scotland*. D. J. Bennet and T. Strang, *The Northwest Highlands*. R. Black, *Mac Mhaighstir Alasdair, the Ardnamurchan Years*. J. M. Boyd and I. M. Boyd, *The Hebrides*. J. M. Bumsted, *The People's Clearance*. R. G. H. Bunce and J. N. R. Jeffers, eds., *Native Pinewoods of Scotland*. John Buchan, *The Marquis of Montrose*. Duncan Campbell, *Lairds of Glen Lyon*. Marion Campbell, *Argyll, The Enduring Heartland*. Hugh Cheape, *Tartan— The Highland Habit*. E. J. Cowan, *Montrose: For Covenant and King*. Joanna Close-Brooks, *Exploring Scotland's Heritage—The Highlands*. T. Clutton-Brock and S. D. Albon, *The Red Deer of the Highlands*. G. Y. Craig, *Geology of Scotland*. R. A. Dodgshon, *Land and Society in Early Scotland*; *The Cultural Landscape* (in J. Birks et al.). F. Fraser Darling and J. Morton Boyd, *The Highlands and Islands*. A. A. M. Duncan, *Scotland, The Making of the Kingdom*. I. Finlay, *Columba*. Gaskell, *Morvern Transformed*. William A. Gillies, *In Famed Breadalbane*. Seton Gordon, *Highways and Byways in the Central Highlands*; *Highways and Byways in the West Highlands*. Robert Graves, *The White Goddess*. I. F. Grant and Hugh Cheape, *Periods in Highland History*. I. Grimble, *The Trial of Patrick Sellar*. A. R. B. Haldane, *The Drove Roads of Scotland*; *New Ways through the Glens*. P. Hudson, *The Red Grouse in Time and Space*. James Hunter, *The Making of the Crofting Community*. Inverness Field Club, *The Seventeenth Century in the Highlands*. H. H. Lamb, *Climate, History and the Modern World*. W. R. Kermack, *The Clan MacGregor*; *The Highlands*. Bruce Lenman, *Jacobite Clans of the Great Glen*. Eric Linklater, *The Black Watch*. Calum MacLean, *The Highlands*. Sir Fitzroy Maclean, *Bonnie Prince Charlie*. Lorraine Maclean of Dochgarroch, *The Middle Ages in the Highlands*. Sorley MacLean, *Spring Tide and Neap Tide: Selected Poems 1932–1972*. A. MacLeod, *The Songs of Duncan Ban Macintyre*. D. N. McVean and D. A. Ratcliffe, *Plant Communities of the Scottish Highlands*. M. Magnusson, *Common Sense and Sustainability, a Partnership for the Cairngorms*. P. Maitland and R. N. Campbell, *Freshwater Fishes*. W. Matheson, *The Blind Harper*. Joseph Mitchell, *Reminiscences of my Life in the Highlands* (2 vols.). I. Moncreiffe of Easter Moncreiffe, *The Robertsons*. W. H. Murray, *Highland Landscape*; *Rob Roy*. Thompson D. Nethersole and A. Watson, *The Cairngorms*. W. F. H. Nicolaisen, *Scottish Place-Names*. C. O'Baoill, *Bardachd Shilis na Ceapaich*. A. C. O'Dell and Kenneth Walton, *The Highlands and Islands of Scotland*. Herman Palsson and Paul Edwards, eds., *The Orkneyinga Saga—The History of the Earls of Orkney*. Peter L. Payne, *The Hydro*. Thomas Pennant, *Journals*. John Prebble, *Glencoe*; *The Highland Clearances*; *Mutiny*. Marchioness of Tullibardine, *A Military History of Perthshire*. A. A. R. Ramsay, *The Arrow of Glen Lyon*. D. A. Ratcliffe, *Nature Conservation Review*. Eric Richards, *History of The Highland Clearances* (2 vols.). G. Ritchie and M. Harman, *Exploring Scotland's Heritage—Argyll and the Western Isles*. G. Ritchie and Anna Ritchie, *Scotland, Archaeology and Early History*. T. C. Smout, *A History of the Scottish People, 1560–1830*. Alfred P. Smyth, *Warlords and Holy Men*. H. M. Steven and A. Carlisle, *The Native Pinewoods of Scotland*. D. Stevenson, *Alisdair MacColla and the Highland Problem of the late Seventeenth Century*. John Stewart of Ardvorlich, *The Camerons*. Usher and D. Thompson, *Ecological Change in the Uplands*. B. Walker and G. Ritchie, *Fife and Tayside*. J. Carmichael Watson, *Gaelic Songs of Mary MacLeod*. W. J. Watson, *Bardachd Gaidhlig*; *Celtic Place Names of Scotland*. T. Weir, *The Scottish Lochs*. Dorothy Wordsworth, *Journal of a Tour . . .* J. B. Whittow, *Geology and Scenery in Scotland*.

I have also consulted numerous papers in 'Scottish Studies' and the 'Transactions of the Gaelic Society of Inverness'; 'Scottish Historical Review', the newsletter of the Native Woodlands Discussion Group; 'Scottish Forestry'; 'Reforesting Scotland'; and articles by Dr Adam Watson and others in the *Shooting Times*.

Acknowledgements

Working on my own at home I have needed to ask for advice from many people on subjects on which they are expert. All have encouraged, advised and informed with characteristic generosity. I am most grateful to them all, and, indeed to anyone whom I have forgotten. Needless to say any mistakes are mine.

Thanks to:
Dr John Bannerman of the Department of Scottish History, Edinburgh University; Mr Robin Callendar; Dr James Fenton of the National Trust for Scotland; Professor William Gillies of the Department of Celtic, Edinburgh University; Mr Gunnar Godwin, formerly of the Forestry Commission; Dr John Gordon of Scottish Natural Heritage; Professor Bruce Lenman of the Department of Modern History, St Andrews University; Mr Simon MacGowan of Perth and Kinross District Library (Blairgowrie); Mr Gordon Maxwell of the Royal Commission on Ancient and Historical Monuments for Scotland; Miss Morag MacLeod of the School of Scottish Studies; Professor Donald McIntyre; Major David McMicking, formerly of the Black Watch; Mr Roger Mercer, Secretary of the Royal Commission on Ancient and Historic Monuments for Scotland; Dr I. Morrison of the Department of Geography, Edinburgh University; Dr Robert Moss of the Institute of Terrestrial Ecology, Banchory; Mr Brendan O'Hanrahan of Scottish Natural Heritage; Mrs Faith Raven, Ardtornish; Mr and Mrs Angus Robertson, Ardtornish Estate; Mr David Sellar of the Department of Scots Law, Edinburgh University; Professor T. C. Smout of the Institute for Environmental History, St Andrews University; Dr Rab Soutar of Forest Enterprise; Mr Gavin Sprott of the National Museum of Scotland; Dr Des Thompson of Scottish Natural Heritage; Mr Andy Wightman of Reforesting Scotland.

Dr Allan Brown of the Countryside Council for Wales; John MacInnes, formerly of the School of Scottish Studies; Adam Watson, formerly of the Institute for Terrestrial Ecology, Banchory and Ian Whyte of the Department of Geography, University of Lancaster, have read the text in various stages, and Mr Niall Campbell, formerly of the Nature Conservancy Council, read some parts of it. My friend Hugh Cheape of the National Museum of Scotland was a constant source of information and guidance. I am indebted also to Pippa Lewis for suggesting to Mark Collins that I might be a suitable author for this book, to Sampson Lloyd for his stunning photographs and to the genial editorship of Colin Ziegler.

Finally, without the constant help of my wife, Louise, I do not suppose that I should have managed to write the book at all.

INDEX